THE POWER

OF THE

Pussy

BY

KARA KING

DISCLAIMER AND/OR LEGAL NOTICES

The information presented herein represents the view of the author as of the date of publication. Due to the rate at which conditions change, the author reserves the right to alter and update her opinion based on new conditions.

This material is general dating advice only and is not intended to be a substitute for professional medical or psychological advice. This book is for entertainment purposes only. This book contains sexually explicit material and is not intended for persons under the age of eighteen (18).

Acknowledgments

To God, whose glory makes all things
possible. To my husband, Jason, you are an
amazing man and a wonderful Father. To my
beautiful mother, Kristy, words aren't enough
to express my gratitude and love for you. To
my life long best friend, Staci, for being the
yin to my yang. To my grandmother, Marvis,
for motivating me when I had almost given
up.

To all the women before me who have gone
against the grain, stood up for our rights,
and served as positive examples to other
young women...

THANK YOU

TABLE OF CONTENTS

Chapter 3

Chapter 4

Chapter 5

Chapter 6

Chapter 7

Chapter 8

Chapter 9

Chapter 10

Chapter 11

Chapter 12

INTRODUCTION

This book will dramatically empower your life as a woman by teaching you valuable secrets that will uncover your natural abilities to control your relationships and have men at your feet.

Once you're able to alter your perception *and* utilize the 12 secret powers, you will feel like a new woman. You will effortlessly break the cycle of bad relationships. You will then find the man of your dreams, make him fall head over heels in love with you, and give you everything you ever wanted!

Every woman has the potential to make this happen. It doesn't matter if you're fat, short, tall, skinny, or shy. You could be a woman who is 18 and single, or 45 and divorced for the third time.

Whoever you are and whatever you're going through, you carry the potential within you to completely change your outcomes with men. I'm sure you've seen an array of examples of women who manage the impossible.

The unattractive woman with the good-looking man that makes you think, "what does he see in her?" The woman you know who's a complete bitch, yet her man is at her beck and call. The women who have men at their disposal, buying them gifts, and never hesitating to treat them like princesses.

Have you ever wondered why some women can effortlessly get men to treat them well, take them on nice dates, buy them things, and remain faithful; while other women struggle with their relationships? What are these women doing that the other women are not doing?

I can tell you these women do not fall into these situations by accident. While some women are able to do this naturally, some women know exactly what they're doing. They intentionally manipulate the male mind by using simple techniques that all women possess. I call these techniques "powers" because they allow us to have great power over men.

All we need to know is what these powers are and how to use them. That's exactly what this book is going to teach you. Unfortunately, many women will go through life without this knowledge. Instead, they will instinctively go with the flow of love, following destiny and fate, only to end up hurt in the end.

Some of us fall for a person so hard, we end up hurt by him repeatedly. Some of us will get hurt by a man, learn from the mistake, only to move onto to another man that ends up hurting us in a completely different way. We end up learning from one heartbreak, only to move onto to the next heart breaker! This happens over and over again until most of us end up with a bitter mind set, believing all men are assholes, users, liars, and cheaters.

Not all men are shit heads, I promise. Honestly, there are some awesome men out there and unbelievably, they're not that hard to find. The old saying, "good men are hard to find", is only true because you cannot "find" a good man. Good men are created.

The challenge isn't in *finding* the good man. The real challenge lies within becoming the woman that makes him *want* to be a good man. Once you have that desire from him, then you have the ultimate opportunity to mold, train, and shape him. Making a man *want* to be dedicated, faithful, and caring takes skill and the powers are going to provide you with that expertise.

I know you are probably thinking, "easier said then done". Surprisingly, this is much easier than it seems! You have the power inside of you, right now, to make a man fall head over heels in love with you, marry you, provide for you, and be faithful to you for life! This book is going to show you how, one chapter at a time.

Whatever it is you seek from a man or from your relationships, you can acquire. Knowledge is power. The game is about to change. You are going to be the one breaking hearts, using men, serial dating, and making men fall for you... instead of the other way around. This is going to be fun and exciting. When it's all over you will feel refreshed, empowered, and excited about dating and being a woman.

The book is broken down into 12 chapters. Each chapter will discuss one of the 12 powers. I will go into detail about each power and how to apply it in real life situations. There will also be assignments you should complete before moving on to the next section. I suggest buying a journal for these assignments, but I have also included them at the end of the book so you can print them out. I will also include resources, helpful links, and other information to help guide you, motivate you, and keep you on track once you are done with the book.

I also need to warn you that I will be very blunt and brutally honest throughout the book. I do not sugar coat anything. I will use curse words and there will be sexually explicit moments throughout the book. This is my way of getting my message across and my own personal writing style.

I'm not here to beat around the bush and be proper, I'm here to empower you. Therefore, I apologize in advance if you are offended at any time during the book. It's my hope that you will appreciate the straight forward "girl talk".

Before we move forward with the book I must ask for three things: Courage. Commitment. Change. Your **commitment** to follow through and your **courage** to **change** will directly reflect your success.

The old ways were not working, so now it is time to change if you want to start experiencing a different outcome with men. You can read this book 100 times, but if you do not have the commitment or the courage to make the changes necessary to utilize the knowledge, then your time and energy will be wasted.

At times, you may find it awkward to put the advice into action. Just realize that this uncomfortable feeling is a part of changing. Be brave enough to embrace the discomfort and move forward. With practice and time, it will all begin to feel normal.

Just like learning to ride a bike, at first it seemed impossible. After a few practice runs, you got the hang of it, and now you can ride a bike with ease. Learning a new style of interacting with men will be the same way.

See, right now you have a certain mind set and attitude towards men and dating. That will have to be completely destroyed and replaced with a new mind set. It's going to be uncomfortable and seem impossible at first, but if you are determined to change your outcomes with men, you will get the hang of it. Before you know it, this will all become second nature to you.

Once you are able let go of previous misconceptions about men, a completely new world awaits you. You will have men lining up to date you, desperate for your attention, and eager to please you. You will never be sad over a man again. You will not be cheated on, lied to, or let down by a man ever again. You will find Mr. Right, make him fall madly in love with you, and never want to leave you. Best of all, you will be having the time of your life while doing it!

Chapter One

THE POWER OF
CONTROLLING YOUR EMOTIONS

This is the first chapter of the book because it will be the hardest of the powers to learn, but it will also be one of your greatest lessons. Learning to use the power of controlling your emotions may possibly be your biggest challenge because it forces you to go against what you're automatically inclined to do, which is to be emotional.

Men are sexual by nature and women are emotional by nature. That's just the way it is. It doesn't matter your race, culture, age, country of origin, or level of education. None of that matters. A woman is a woman. We are all different, but inside we operate the same. We're emotional creatures.

We think with our hearts and we act on emotion. It's a natural and completely normal part of being a female. It's what makes us great mothers. It enables us to care for the ones we love without effort. We're natural born nurturers. It's going to be a difficult task to try to control what comes naturally, but we can evolve. You must evolve if you want to beat men at their own game. **You must learn to control your emotions.**

Here's the thing...there's nothing at all wrong with being emotional. It's normal. We just need to realize the tremendous benefit of knowing when to hold back on emotion and when to let it go. It's not necessary to go to the extreme of becoming a cold-hearted bitch with no feelings. **It is necessary, however, to become aware of your emotions and their ability to control your actions. Once we're aware of this fact, then we can control our actions by controlling our emotions.**

When you master the ability to control your emotions, you take away a man's power over you. While it may be technically "wrong" to mask and control your emotions for your own selfish benefit, it's simply a necessity you must accept in order to win the game. In my opinion there's nothing wrong with this type of "hide your feelings" mentality, because if you think about it, guys do it to us all the time!

We're so used to their blatant lying, manipulative, dog-like ways that we've become numb to it. We think it's "wrong" that they dog us out, but that doesn't stop us from getting sucked into their traps time after time. So, whether it's wrong or right, you have to flip the emotional switch on men. It's a necessity and here's why…

The Most Important Thing You Need to Know About Men

Since the beginning of time there has been a particular type of man. I'm talking about the kind of man that has women figured out. He's perfected the art of playing with a woman's mind. These type of guys know how to manipulate, lie, cheat, hurt, use, and break hearts with no remorse. Even worse is their ability to keep women around, even after they've done all of those terrible things! How did they get so good at it? They know our weakness: our emotions...

Many men are too stupid to even realize they're doing this. We make it that easy for them! However, some men do know what they're doing. These are the worst. You must be on the look out; aware and cautious. They're like predators stalking prey. These are the players, the cheaters, the users, the pimps, the douche bags and the all around assholes.

These men know how to use a woman's emotions for their own personal gain, whatever that may be. It could be sex, money, clothes, or simply a place to live. You have to be conscious of this fact: **There are men out there that will do and say anything just to get what they need.** Once they get what they want, it's time to move on. They know good and well they're going to hurt you, but they simply don't care. They easily walk away, while you are left devastated. They're heartless, cruel, and calculated.

I'm not saying *all* men are like this. But, you must be aware that there's a lot more bad guys than you think and they're everywhere. They know how to use a woman's emotions against her by telling her in the most sincere ways just exactly what she wants to hear.

They'll play that game as long as it takes in order to drain you of whatever it is they want out of you. Then they leave or perhaps they string you along for as long as you're willing to take it. **<u>You must be wise to this fact.</u>** Don't get sucked into their traps. Just as you're about to be educated on how to get what you want from men, these guys know how to get what they want from women.

We don't even realize it, but our emotions have made us easy targets. Our emotions have caused us to do things we would never do. Have you ever looked back at one of your previous relationships and wondered, "What the hell was I thinking?" Of course, you have. We've all been down that road. The thing to realize is that you weren't thinking at all. You were acting on emotions.

You were reacting to feelings when you needed to be controlling them. Simply put, you were acting with your heart, instead of listening to your head. Sounds romantic and it seems like that's what you're supposed to do for love, but it's actually the worst thing you can do. Unless, you enjoy being a fool in love. But if you want to be a strong woman who doesn't have issues with men, it's a huge mistake. Therefore, I ask that you forget about romance and going with your feelings. Those days are gone (for now).

The only way you're going to get ahead of the game is to get a grip on your feelings. You have to know who's boss. Is it your emotions or your brain? It should be an easy choice, your brain, of course! But it's not easy. We are women, hard-wired to think with our hearts.

Here's a classic scenario. A guy just broke your heart in two, stomped on it, and walked away as if it was no big deal. A logical person would give him the finger and move on, but not emotional creatures like us. No way! We ask ourselves 100 times, "Why is he doing this to me?" We make a dozen different excuses as to why his behavior is forgivable. Then we plot out all of the ways we're going to get him back. We even do all of this when we know he's a piece of shit and we should let him go.

This is a huge problem! **Allowing our emotions to influence our actions and decisions is what gets us into trouble.** It serves no purpose whatsoever. It may give short-term satisfaction, but it always leads to greater heartache. Controlling your emotions is the most important thing to do during two different phases. At the *beginning* of relationships and at the *end* of relationships. I want to start with the hardest one: the end of relationships.

Controlling Your Emotions at the End of Relationships

Your man just hurt you. Again. You know he's no good and you should just break up with him and move on. However, you can't stop thinking about him. You grovel, you cry, you think, think, think and then think some more. You want to call him, send him a text, or talk to his friends. You may even allow him a chance to beg for forgiveness or give him an opportunity to win you back; even when you know you he's not good for you.

We only do these irrational actions so our emotional side can "feel better." We give in to our emotions in order to feel better in the short term, but we end up hurting even more over the long term. Even the strongest women have made stupid decisions based on their inability to control their emotions.

We've all taken back men when we knew we shouldn't have. We're only trying to make ourselves feel better, so we end up making stupid decisions based on hurt feelings. This is why so many of us take the loser back repeatedly. It's just our emotional, feminine, loving side controlling our brains. That's why you can't think or act logically when it comes to leaving a man that you love, but you know is no good for you. Here's how you can get the strength…

The Easy Part:

Recognizing When You're Reacting to Emotion

It's easy to notice when this is happening because you know deep in your heart that you're making a bad decision. You know when you're taking too much shit from a man. It's also easy to recognize when this is happening because your friends and family are telling you to leave him alone, but you're not listening! It's easy to *recognize* when the emotions are making you a fool. The hard part is once you recognize it, you have to *control* it.

The Hard Part:

Controlling Your Reaction

This is where the work comes in. Although you

can't stop the emotions, **you can control how you respond to them**. Who's running the show here, your emotions or you? You're the one in control. Your heart may be broken and you really want to forgive this man, but you *can* stop yourself.

You *must* stop yourself! You can say to yourself, "I know I'm terribly sad right now and there's nothing I want more than to be back with him. But, I realize that's my emotions talking and I've decided that this time I'm not going to do what my emotions want me to do."

The Hardest Part:

The Feelings Are Still There and They Really Hurt

Even though you've made a choice not to react to the pain, your heart will still be broken. The pain will still be there. The sadness will be constantly present. However, if you can just control yourself, it will eventually go away. It takes some time. You have to occupy yourself and your mind until it goes away.

Help For a Broken Heart

The final and most important step to controlling emotions is treating your broken heart and hurt feelings *just like a wound*. Give them time to heal. It hurts at first, but as time goes by, it will get less and less painful. Our biggest problem is that we're impatient. We don't want to wait around for it to heal. We want that heart fixed NOW!

Rather than allowing it to heal, we do all kinds of stupid, irrational things to make it feel better. I know how bad it hurts. It feels like a constant pain in your chest and stomach. You feel sick to your stomach and you can't stop thinking about it. It physically hurts. You want to throw up. You can't eat. You can't sleep. It can put you into a deep depression and at its very worst...it has led people to suicide. Dealing with this type of pain isn't easy. It can seem impossible to get through, but you can do this!

You have to do this. Because you know if you give in to the emotions and take the man back or beg him back in an effort to feel better; won't the pain come back again eventually? Won't this person just do this again? Won't the cycle just continue? It's best to move on now and allow yourself to go through the healing process, rather than repeating the same painful emotional roller coaster.

The Most Important Part:

You Have to Get Distracted

So, the feelings are still there and it's going to hurt. Now what? How do you move on? Occupy your mind during this painful time. It's the most important thing you can do. Go out with your friends, get a dog, get a second job. **Do whatever it takes to get your mind focused on**

something other than him. Many women join the gym and start dieting during this time. Not only does it occupy your mind, but you'll look great when it's all said and done.

You'll think about him while out with your friends. You'll think about him when you're at your second job, at the gym, or while playing with your new puppy. That's okay, that's normal. As long as you aren't picking up the phone and calling him. As long as you're not allowing him to come over and "work things out."

You're going to continue to feel the pain, you're just distracting your mind and re-directing your thoughts until the pain heals. It may take a few weeks or a few months, but the pain will eventually get less and less intense. Then, I promise, eventually the pain will go away.

Once the pain is gone, congratulate yourself! You've just utilized the power of controlling your emotions! This means you have the ability to walk away from any man for any reason! No man will ever have power or control over you or be able to use your emotions against you. This is a really BIG DEAL!

Let's Review How to Control Emotions:

1) Recognize that because you're a woman, you're naturally inclined to react on emotion. (There's nothing wrong with that fact, we just need to recognize that we can greatly benefit from knowing when and how to control it.)

2) Now that you know this, never make decisions based on your emotions!!!

3) Recognize the emotions/feelings/pain will still be there.

4) You're not going to give into it this time, because you are in control.

5) You're going to give your emotions the time they need to heal. If you have a wound on your knee, do you keep picking at it? No. You wrap it up and leave it alone until it heals. Your emotions are no different.

6) Most importantly, occupy yourself while you heal. You'll still think of him, but you'll be too busy to give in to calls and visits.

NEVER EVER

Grovel Over a Man!

If he hasn't been treating you the way you deserve or want to be treated…let him go. Don't allow your emotions to put you into a position to be used or hurt. I know your heart feels pain and your emotions tell you to call him, run after him, or go see if his car is parked at home (we've all done it). Nevertheless, out of respect and dignity for yourself, learn to have control. ***DO NOT CALL HIM, DO NOT CONTACT HIM, LEAVE HIM ALONE FOREVER***. He screwed up and now he must pay the consequence: He lost YOU.

It's very hard to get over rejection or a broken heart. I don't expect you not to "feel the pain." It will still be there. All day and all night, your heart will ache. That's the point! Whether or not you continue to force this toxic relationship to work, you will *still* feel the pain! Why not feel the pain while doing something productive; rather than chase, stalk, grovel, wonder, worry or cry over your guy?

Filler Dates

A good way to keep busy and distract your mind from heartache is to start dating again. Even if you're so heartbroken, you have absolutely no desire to date. Don't date for the sake of dating. Date to distract your heart from the pain. Usually while our hearts are broken, dating is the last thing we want to think about because our minds are too consumed with grief. But it's actually the most critical time to start dating. Don't resist dating during the one time when you really need the distraction.

Overwhelming thoughts about your ex or the fact that you feel nothing toward your date are completely normal. Don't let this detour you from this great mental escape. Being a woman, you have the right to go out on dates, even if you don't intend to be with the man. So, don't worry about that.

Go on a few "Filler Dates." I call them "Filler Dates" because these are dates you use to fill your time, mind, or heart. You may go on a filler date because you're bored and you would like to go out to a nice dinner. You may want to go on a filler date because you just got dumped, and can't keep your mind off your ex. You might feel sad throughout the whole date, but that's four more hours you haven't called your ex!

Filler dates aren't wrong because a man is taking you on a date with an intention to try to convince you to "try him out." It's like a sales pitch, you don't have to buy anything. You're just there to see if you might be interested. Granted, you may not be attracted or interested, but you're giving him the chance. Sometimes men are just happy for the chance.

Men are a lot less complex than we are. They want you because you have a vagina. They don't mind gambling their money on your dinner and a movie just to see if they have a chance. Okay, maybe they mind when the date is over and they get NOTHING, but fuck that, you don't owe him anything. Your presence was enough.

Again, don't feel bad about this. Men use us all the time. You're using filler dates for your own benefit, just as a man would easily use a woman for sex. Don't feel guilty. Control those emotions of guilt and move forward.

Filler dates are dates used to fill your time, make you feel better, and to be reminded of just how much men are interested in you. When you have men pursuing you, even if you don't like them, you'll start to realize this other loser is missing out on something. **Filler dates are a tool to help you recuperate from a broken heart by taking your mind off the wound as it heals.** I'll talk more about filler dates and how to have men lining up to date you in Chapter Ten.

Things I Hate About You

If you're having a really tough time getting over a guy, another tool you can use is the "Things I Hate About You" list. Grab your journal and write down all of the things that bothered you about this person. Write down the things you hated about him. From the big things like, "he's a liar and a cheater" to the small things like, "the mole on his back."

Whatever it is that grossed you out, pissed you off, and aggravated you about this man needs to be written down on that list. I don't care how insignificant it is, write it down. When you're having a hard day, pull out the list, read it and laugh. You may need to read it everyday or several times a day. Eventually, you'll get to a point where you'll sit back and laugh, wondering what you ever saw in this lying, mole-filled asshole.

The "Things I Hate About You List" and "Filler Dates" are two tools you now have to gain control of your emotions and move through a broken heart. However, it's not only important to control your emotions for the sake of a broken heart. You need to have control on the other end of a relationship...the beginning.

Controlling Emotions in the Beginning of Relationships

Controlling your emotions is also important when you meet or like a new guy. You know, like when you want to call him, text him, or leave comments on his Facebook page. Or when you're waiting for him to call, like he said he would and so you decide to call him.

You *know* you should just wait it out and let him come to you, but you're dying to reach out to him. Don't do it! Be patient. Control yourself. Always wait it out and always make them come to you. If he doesn't, that's a SURE SIGN he doesn't like you.

How to Tell If a Guy Likes You

If a guy likes you, he WILL pursue you. If he doesn't, then he doesn't like you. No excuses. You'll need to learn to accept this fact. Don't pursue men. Control those emotions that urge you to go after men!

Yes, even if he's shy. Yes, even if he doesn't know you like him. It's okay to flirt. Just don't pursue. Be patient.

If he likes you, he'll call. If he likes you, he'll text. If he likes you, he'll find ways to be around you. If he doesn't, take it as his way of letting you know that he isn't interested.

Women should never have to put a lot effort into getting a man's attention. If you're not getting the responses, calls, texts, or attention you were hoping for, then forget about him. He most likely doesn't like you, or he'd show it and you would know it.

There's a book called, *He's Just Not That Into You*. I suggest EVERY single woman read this book, if you haven't already. It helps with grasping the fact that if a guy isn't calling, texting, flirting, or actively pursuing you; then **he's just not that into you**. Too many of us sit around by the phone waiting for a guy to call back or ask us out on another date, only to get let down when he doesn't. We make excuses for them, get our feelings hurt, and even worse we blame ourselves. That book's brutal honesty will help you see those crappy situations for what they really are.

Here are three reasons why you must control your emotions when meeting a new guy or in the beginning of a relationship:

Reason #1:
Men hate it when they can't see into your head. If you control your emotions for a new guy, you're making him wonder if you like him or not. When he can't figure it out,

he'll work harder. Suddenly, he'll be the one calling and texting. He'll be the one pursuing you, instead of the other way around.

Reason #2:

Men only want you when you don't want them. It's all about the thrill of the hunt for a man. I know you've heard this before and probably think it's just stupid bullshit games. To us, it's stupid because we're women, our brains are different. We think, "hey, if you like me, then be with me."

Men aren't like that. Men want to hunt. The thrill of the hunt gets a man interested much faster than calling him and leaving cute comments on his Facebook page. That's just the way it is. The sooner you accept this, the better for you. Flirt with him, but control your urge to go after him and *if* he likes you, he'll definitely come after you.

Reason #3:

Only fools rush in. As women, we get swept off our feet too easily. Don't be so quick to like a new guy, especially one you just met or just started dating. Control those happy emotions that come so easily in the beginning of relationships. Don't go on one or two dates with some guy and immediately start getting feelings for him or start thinking he's the one. Slow down. Control yourself and play hard to get.

The Phone Trick

Here's a tactic you can use in the beginning of a relationship or when you first start talking to a guy: Be the one to get off the phone at least two out of three times. Do this until the relationship has developed. Have excuses or reasons to get off of the phone before conversations begin. You don't need to do it every time, but you should be the one getting off of the phone a majority of the time.

Have your conversations and talk as you normally would, but don't be the one willing to talk to him, as long as he's willing to talk to you. Cut the conversation in a polite and apologetic way. This is subconsciously letting him know that you don't need him to entertain you. It also tells him you're a busy woman that doesn't need to cling on to men. More importantly, it makes him wonder if you like him and it makes him look forward to talking to you again.

Make This Promise to Yourself

You must promise yourself that from this day forward you're taking responsibility for YOUR actions. The things you do for men, which you later think, "What the hell was I thinking?" are not his fault. They are your fault. These foolish notions will no longer happen if you're able to maintain composure over your feelings. They are your emotions and you must learn to control them by not allowing them to dictate your actions. When you do, you will take the lead when dealing with men and you'll be the one calling the shots.

Controlling your emotions is an extremely valuable tool that will help you gain control over your relationships; whether that means you're leaving your ex for good, or meeting a new guy that you really like. ***REMEMBER!* A strong, confident woman still feels pain, still wants to call the guy she likes, but she doesn't. She controls those emotions, and therefore, controls the relationships she has with men.**

So far, we've learned that men use our emotions against us. Good news is that there's an even playing ground! What kind of weapons of love do women get? It's so obvious and simple, but we rarely ever know we have it, yet alone how to use it to our advantage. Our weapon is sex. Our vaginas, breasts, hips, legs, and our asses are to men what emotions are to us. Sex is their greatest weakness. Mwahahahahaha...

Chapter Two

THE POWER OF THE PUSSY

Being a girl is an absolute blessing! When a woman realizes that what she has in between her legs gives her great power, she can get whatever she wants. Once you know how to work what you've got, life becomes easier. Suddenly, you have the control. You can get anything you want from men, once you learn how to use your pussy to your advantage.

Women who realize their vagina is valuable will always have the upper hand. When you start to respect and value your vagina, so will the men in your life. Once they see you're a woman who knows the value of her pussy, they will either back off because they know they can't handle (aka afford) a girl like you or they'll give you your asking price, whatever that may be.

I always laugh when I hear a man say, "If I was a girl, I'd be rich!". They say this because THEY KNOW women have the ultimate ability to manipulate men. It could be love and commitment, a house and diamonds, or all of the above! **What do *YOU* want from men?**

Take this time to write down exactly what you want to accomplish with men. What do you really want from men that you've been unable to get? Is it commitment? Honesty? Gifts? Dates? Marriage? Respect? Money? A variety of these things? What exactly do you want?

Think hard about this and then write it down. (We'll get back to this list in a minute.) Whatever it is you desire, your pussy can obtain it for you. By the end of this chapter, you will have learned the fine art of using pussy to set your demands and get exactly what you want.

The Hot Commodity

Pussy is a commodity. Men wouldn't pay for it, if it didn't have value. You could throw pussy on the stock market and it would trade with the diamonds and gold. Even better than diamonds and gold, pussy has the magical ability to have a drastic price range. Pussy can range from free, all the way to millions of dollars.

This has nothing to do with prostitution! I'm not telling you to "sell sex." What I'm saying is that you must decide exactly what you want from a man (the stuff on your list). This is your "asking price" and you don't settle for anyone until they are willing to give you your "asking price." When they're willing to give you what you want, then you can "sell."

When I use the term "sell," I'm referring to that moment when you decide to give your heart to a man. That moment when you decide you're going to be in a relationship with a man. Wives of faithful men put a price tag of "honesty and faithfulness," and didn't sell until they were sure they had a faithful and honest man. Wives of wealthy men put a price tag of "luxury and financial security," and didn't sell until they got their asking price.

Until you get what you want, you're still on the market. Don't settle for men that are unwilling to pay the price for your love and affection!

Aren't you worth it?

Women with great husbands didn't get these kinds of guys because they were lucky. They knew what they deserved and they didn't settle until they got it. You can give it away free, or for whatever price you decide it's worth.

Men Need Us, We Don't Need Them

The power of the pussy is powerless without the desperate need from a man. Men NEED sex. They think about it all the time. They crave pussy the way we crave commitment and affection. That's why they'll do all kinds of stupid things to get it.

Their need for sex is a great weakness. Combine that weakness with your pussy, and you are now armed with your *greatest weapon*. Don't feel bad about it. They prey on our emotions. We're going to prey on their need for sex.

See, we don't necessarily *need* to have sex. Sure, we love sex too and we want to have a good time. But let's be honest. It's not a desperate need for us, like it is for them.

Think I'm wrong? How often do you see women paying male hookers for sex? Virtually never. Compare the amount of female strip clubs to male strip clubs, and the numbers are probably a 40 to 1 ratio. Compare the amount of pornography geared towards a male audience versus a female audience and it becomes clear. Most men are much hornier than we'll ever understand.

Did you know that if a man doesn't ejaculate, he will eventually start to feel a mental build up from not having sex? It has to get out! He may jack off and that will suffice for a while, but eventually he is going to feel an INTENSE NEED to have sex. Meanwhile, we could avoid sex for months and it wouldn't bother us nearly as much. **This is our advantage.**

Unfortunately, women tend to flip this around and get it backwards. We do the exact opposite and end up giving sex away easily. We think up all kinds of reasons why it's okay to go ahead have sex with a guy. (We've all been through this at some point or another. I'm not judging anyone.)

Some women simply think sex is the only way to get a man. Some women want to have sex with a guy they like because there's all of this great chemistry. She convinces herself it's okay to rush into it because both are consenting adults in a moment of passion.

Some women think they can hook a man with their great sex, foolishly believing he'll want to be with her because she's the nastiest and freakiest woman he ever met. Then there are the women that say they're just having sex "for fun" and they don't care about the guy, but then secretly get sad when he doesn't call anymore.

Whatever type of girl you may be and whatever your reasoning is, having sex with a guy you like is the absolute WRONG thing to do. The trick is DO NOT HAVE SEX. The less a man gets, the more a man wants. Men only want you when they can't have you. Bottom line. I know it's so stupid and you're probably tired of hearing this. You may think, "If two people like each other, then what's the problem?" Remember... these are men we're dealing with!

To try to understand the illogical mind of a man, I asked men some questions to give you a better understanding of why they make no sense. I interviewed ten single men, ages 18-43, and asked a very specific question, "Why do guys act like they want a girl to give it up, but then treat her badly when she does?" Their answers were brutally honest. They simply said, "Men don't love sluts."

Men Don't Love Sluts

One man was kind enough to elaborate, "They want a girl to give in easily and have sex with them, because ultimately sex is what they want. However, the girl that gives in is the loser in the end. It doesn't matter how good in bed she is or how sexy she is. It doesn't matter how perfect she looks. She's officially a slut because she gave the guy what he wanted and he didn't have to put in any **EFFORT**."

Basically, men *pretend* they want a woman who

"doesn't play games" and is "mature," but these are just bullshit lines to get you to go to bed with them. Men have no problem being sweet in the beginning to get you into bed. They'll even love it while it's happening. However, once the sexual act is complete, the girl disgusts the man. That's why they act differently afterward. Men don't love sluts. They don't even like them.

The woman they really want is the one who rejects them. They want to get the girl that's a challenge and doesn't give it up easily. The girl that makes him wait for it, work for it, and chase after it. The woman he falls in love with is the exact opposite of a slut, because men don't fall in love with sluts.

Men fall in love with ladies. Ladies who are mature enough to know they don't have to have sex. Ladies who don't even want to have sex quickly, because it's an unladylike thing to do. The type of woman a man will love gives off a vibe that says loud and clear: "I'm not an easy girl and you're going to have to put in some effort if you want a girl like me, because I'm very special."

It's the old theory that if you get something for free, you won't appreciate it as much as if you had to work for it. What happens when you give a kid an expensive toy the first time he asks for it without making him earn it? He'll play with it once or twice and then toss it to the side with no further interest.

On the other hand, make a kid beg for the toy for a few weeks. Make the kid prove he deserves the toy with good behavior. Then make the kid do chores to earn the money to buy the toy. By the time the kid finally gets the toy, he's going to love the toy, take good care of it, and appreciate it. Men are like little boys with their toys. Make them wait, make them work, make them pay, and then they will love you, appreciate you, and take good care of you.

What If He Leaves?

Women make a huge mistake by fearing if they hold out on sex, he's going to find another girl or lose interest. If you do hold out on sex and he does lose interest: **GOOD!** He was just out to fuck you and forget you, so aren't you glad you didn't give him any? I'm serious.

If you deny a man sex and
he doesn't continue to pursue you
after you have rejected him;
that is concrete proof he was never genuinely interested in
YOU.

~He was only looking for SEX.~

Don't try to convince yourself it was anything less than him trying to **use you**. When you're out in the dating world, this is going to happen... a lot. So, don't take it personally when it happens. You have to take it for what it is: Men out there having a good time at our expense. You can choose to fall into the category of "women who *can* be used," or the category of "women who *cannot* be used." The choice is completely up to you.

On the other hand, if you're dating a man that takes your rejection like a gentleman and is willing to wait, this is a sign he genuinely likes you for you. Now, if you're just beginning to date and you're not officially committed, there's a chance he still may have someone on the side. In all honesty, he's most likely going to get sex somewhere else if he's not getting it from you. This is still **GOOD!**

How can this possibly be a good thing? While he's using some other woman for sex, he's thinking about you and what it will take to get you to be his girl. She'll be the quick piece of ass and you'll be the woman that gives him butterflies in his stomach. He'll use her for sex, while you're receiving flowers and going out on nice dates. She'll be the one hurt in the end, while you'll be "the one" who made him fall in love.

If you have issues with giving in to sex too easily or you're having a hard time grasping the fact your pussy is a hot commodity, read the page below to yourself. Put it up on your wall, read it every day or write it 100 times until you memorize it. Do whatever is necessary to sink the following statements into your head permanently:

Pretend your vagina is worth something of VALUE.

Pretend it's a $500 bill.

Would you give a man you just met a FREE $500 bill?

Of course, you wouldn't.

NEVER GIVE AWAY YOUR MOST PRECIOUS ASSET FOR FREE!

You MUST realize that what you have in between your legs is a valuable tool to get men to do whatever you want them to do. Your vagina is the ultimate power! She will help you manipulate men and get them to bend over backwards at your will. Respect her. She's your new best friend.

However, there's a catch. There's always a catch. The power of the pussy doesn't work on all men. The catch is that the man has to like you or feel some type of attraction to you for your powers to work on him. But we all know it doesn't take much to get a man's attention. A little bit of flirting and flaunting your femininity goes a long way. (Note: this is not the same as pursuing a man, this is flirting and flaunting. There is a difference.)

Giving up sex easily is the exact **wrong** way to use the power, because it renders you powerless. Number one, you'll lose the power of knowing the guy's true intentions with you. Number two, you'll kill your opportunity to become the woman he falls for.

Now, if you don't like the guy or you don't care to develop a relationship with him, then have sex with him. It won't matter. But, if you really like him and hope to create a committed relationship with this man, then do not have sex with him. The **correct** way to use the power of the pussy is to not allow any man access to it until he has **earned** the right. I will say it again, because it's SO important:

THE CORRECT WAY TO USE THE POWER OF YOUR PUSSY IS TO NOT GIVE IT UP FREELY.

A MAN MUST EARN THE RIGHT TO HAVE SEX WITH YOU.

HE MUST PUT FORTH EFFORT TO PROVE HE IS WORTHY OF YOU.

****

When Has He Earned It?

Now, don't get me wrong. I'm not saying you should go out and become a born again virgin or practice celibacy. You don't need to hold out *that* long. To determine when it's the right time to have sex with a man, you must give him two tests to find out if he's truly worthy of you.

Test #1 - Test his true feelings by making him wait. Wait at least 60 days. Two months is the least amount of time you should wait before having sex. If he's stuck around after you have rejected him and he waited patiently for two months or longer, he's proven that he's not trying to use you.

Test # 2 - Now that he has waited patiently, it's time for the Prince Charming test!

The Prince Charming Test

This test is all about observing your man's actions. Will he run to your rescue when you call? Will he be your Prince Charming? When a man likes a woman, he'll jump through hoops to help her and he'll be glad to come to her rescue.

Actions speak louder than words, so you want to find out what his actions say about his feelings towards you. *If he is easily willing to come to your aide on a consistent basis, this is proof he genuinely cares for you.* You can perform this test in a variety of ways. The options are limitless. The basic rules to implement the test are simple:

Step 1) Put yourself into a position of needing to be rescued or saved or you can just wait until an opportunity arises.

Examples of Situations Requiring Rescue:

-Car breaks down

-Locked out of car

-Need a ride to work for a few days

-Need the car jumped

-Need your car fixed

-Need your lawn mowed

-Need someone to give your Mom a ride

Any situation where you would want a potential mate to be there for you is a situation you can use to test him. Once you're in the situation, you'll need to call your man and find out if he'll be there for you. This is very important. You don't want to get involved with a man that isn't willing to be your Prince Charming. Let's see if he can pass the test.

Step 2) You're going to contact your man to come help you. First things first, call him at a time when you know he can talk. Like, don't call the poor guy in the middle of his weekly meeting at work and expect him to pick up. However, if you call him at a good time, he better pick up the phone. When a man really likes a woman, he'll pick up her calls, return her messages, or call her back quickly. If he sends you to voice mail, doesn't answer and/or doesn't call you back right away, don't make excuses for him. Take it for what it is: Proof that he's not genuinely interested in you.

If you leave a voice mail and let him know your situation and he still doesn't call back, he probably isn't interested in you. At this point, you can know wholeheartedly that this guy probably isn't such a great guy after all. His actions are speaking to you loud and clear. Now, if he does pick up the phone…

Step 3) Observe. How does he handle the situation? Does he offer to help? Does he sound concerned? Does he run to your rescue? Does he tell you he has to go and can't help right now? Does he tell you to call someone else instead? What does he do? How does he act? What do his ACTIONS say about his feelings for you?

Bottom line: Is he coming to your rescue? When a man likes a woman a lot, he will want to rush to her side to be the man that solves her problems. Only you can observe his behaviors and make that decision. Has this man passed The Prince Charming Test?

Once these two tests have been passed, then you know it's probably safe to allow him access to your precious asset, but only if you want to! You're always encouraged to wait longer. The longer the wait, the more he appreciates! However, before you allow him access, you need to have "the talk." We'll get to that in a moment.

Why Make A Man Wait?

-Patience is a virtue very few men possess these days. So, when you find a man who's willing to wait patiently for you, this speaks a lot about his character as a man.

-It lets a man know that you won't be used for sex.

-It weeds out all of the men that are just trying to use you for sex.

-It makes the man you really like respect you.

-It makes the guy you like work harder, because he can't figure out what it takes to get you.

-It's FUN to watch men jump through hoops to try to get you.

-More importantly, it puts the power in your hands. By not having sex, you are the one in control.

DO NOT TELL ANYONE YOUR 60 DAY RULE

If you tell a guy you have a 60-day rule, he's going to stick it out just for the sex. If you tell your friends, there's a chance they might tell on you! This 60-day rule is **your secret**. These types of rules have been around for a long time. Many women practice a 90-day rule or some other personal time line. Some women wait six months or more!

I understand two months is a long time to wait nowadays. We live in a fast-paced society where people meet and have sex in the same day. Well, that's them and not you. You're a lady, and you wait at least two months (or more) for a man to prove to you he's worthy of having sex with you. If you feel you can't wait that long, for whatever reason, then at the very least perform the Prince Charming Test.

I also understand you have needs. If your needs are that intense and you just have to have sex, then you have other options. I'm going to give you two options so you have no excuse to go out and screw a guy you like quicker than 60 days. Sometimes women just need to have sex. I understand; but there is a time, a place, and a way to solve that small issue.

Go buy a vibrator, if you don't already have one. Especially, if you don't have one! Every woman needs one. Too embarrassed to go buy one? Order one discreetly online. I personally order from www.adamandeve.com because they have everything a girl could want. There's also an instant $10 off coupon when you sign up for email alerts.

You could also make it a girl's day out kind of thing and plan a trip to the sex store with your best friend. You will have a blast laughing with your friend in the store. Give it a try one day. Or perhaps, have a close friend go buy one for you. If that doesn't work for you and/or you really just want to have sex, then have a "fuck buddy" or a "friend with benefits."

This fuck friend has to be someone you keep separate from your real life. He's just there for those times when you need a man. If keeping him around will keep you from screwing your date on the first or second night, then by all means, you need a friend with benefits. However, under no circumstance are you to think about any kind of future relationship with him!

Men Are Hoes Too

I want to open you up to a whole new way of looking at men. From now on when you meet men, you are going to put them into one of two categories: He's either potential husband material or he's a ho. One or the other. Not all men are boyfriend or husband material; these are your hoes.

I don't mean ho by the traditional "cash for sex" meaning. I call them hoes because these are men you use for sex, money, or to entertain you on a lonely night. However, potential husband material gets respect and you act like a lady around him.

Don't feel guilty about this, ladies! This is how men look at us, so we're just flipping it around and using their own tactics against them. Ha ha! Start categorizing men from now on. The man you like a lot or the good men that are potential relationships, you don't have sex with. The hoes you use. It's that simple. Keep the two separated.

You Can't Turn a Ho Into a Husband

Having hoes comes with responsibilities and rules:

Rule #1:

Hoes are there for *YOU*.
You aren't there for them or for their entertainment, so keep your hoes in control.

Rule #2:

Don't catch feelings. Don't get emotionally involved or emotionally attached.

Rule #3:

Hoes are secrets. Keep them on the down low. They're separate from your normal life. None of the other men in your life need to know you have a ꜱuddy. Believe me, most of the men you date probably have one too, and they won't be telling you about it!

Rule #4:

Don't feel bad about this!!!

I know some of you are feeling guilty just thinking about this. Stop it! Men do this to us all the time. You have to be able to move past the guilt. Society dictates that we should be mindful little women, while men run around acting like animals.

Fuck that.

As long as you're practicing safe sex, being responsible, and you're a single woman... why feel guilty? It's YOUR life and YOUR vagina. If you aren't committed to anyone, then you aren't doing anything wrong. Besides, men don't mind being used for sex.

"The Talk"

When you do get involved with a man you like that patiently waited and passed your Prince Charming test; you may be ready to move forward with your relationship. However, you need to have "The Talk" *before* you have sex. This may be one of the most important conversations you have with this man.

You can only have this conversation during that imperative time frame *before* having sex and *after* making him work so hard for it. This is *your* moment. Whatever it is that you want from this man, at this point in your relationship, now is the time to ask. You're going to ask in a nice, sweet, feminine, and sexy way.

This is when you need to get everything out on the table; slowly, clearly, and sweetly. It's time to discuss monogamy, the status of your relationship, or whatever it is you desire from him. If you want this man to be your boyfriend and it's not obvious that you're his girlfriend, **NOW** is the time to discuss this. This is the time to **ASK** for what you want.

See, I have a theory. Women have PMS, but men have PEAK and PES. PES is Post Ejaculation Syndrome. It's that little attitude change they get after they bust a nut.

You know, when they become little assholes because they got what they wanted.

On the other hand, when they get all sweet because they want it, that's called PEAK. PEAK is Pre-Ejaculation Ass Kissing. **It's during PEAK that we have the most power.** Take advantage of PEAK! PEAK makes men do cRaZZzY things! Just like PMS makes us do crazy shit. Hormones are a bitch.

"The Talk" is basically your first round of PEAK with this man. You can get a lot of what you want during PEAK, so don't be afraid to tell a man what you want or expect. He's either going to say yes or no.

If he denies you what you want, then you tell him "access denied" and move on to the next man. Chances are, however, that if he likes you and he's in PEAK mode, you're going to get every last thing you ask for.

Keep in mind, you have to be ready to ask for what you want, but you also have to be willing to cut your losses if he isn't willing to give you what you want. Because you know what, there are plenty of men out there ready and willing to give you exactly what you want. You just haven't met them yet.

"Just Say It"

Never assume that a man knows what you want or

need. He doesn't. Remember when I said men are not as complex as we are? They are very simple. Once you understand this, it makes a world of difference. You should remember that men are so simple, that when you need to talk to them about something you should JUST SAY IT.

Don't beat around the bush. Don't sit quietly with an attitude or make slick comments in an attempt to get him to realize there's a problem. Just say what you want to say. Even if you're mad or he pissed you off somehow, just let him know by communicating in a sexy way, not a bitchy, nagging way.

A man can't deny a woman's commands if she's turning him on while she's making them! This method of communication is almost like hypnotizing men, they lose focus and easily give in to your every whim. That pussy is powerful!

If you want him to ask you out, say it! If you want to be exclusive, say it! Simply and sweetly say, "I was wondering when you're going to ask me to be your girlfriend?" Simple as that. If the guy you like doesn't call enough, say it! If you like his sweet texts in the morning, say it!!! Okay...I think you get my point.

So, the next time you want something from a man, test my theory. Wait until you are in a PEAK moment, like when he has dimmed the lights and he's trying to rub your back and get you in the mood or what not. Give him some kisses, rub his arms, and then look at him with that horny look in your eyes and sweetly say; "I don't like when you go days without calling me. I wish you'd call me every day."

Always maintain that sweet, sexy tone and stray far away from a bitchy, nagging tone. I understand sometimes you just want to curse them out and you just need to fight. I get it. You can't maintain the sexy composure every time. However, you'll find that by doing this a majority of the time, you'll get a lot more of what you want from men.

They don't pay attention to our hints, our passive aggressive behavior, our attitudes, and our clues as to what our beef is. When we do those things, they honestly don't notice there's a problem. Yes, they really are that clueless. When you realize how clueless they truly can be, you'll see how easy it is to get what you want.

If you want to be his girlfriend, you need to make this known **BEFORE** you have sex, during PEAK. However, don't ask him to be your boyfriend. Simply and politely make it known you're not willing to move forward without that commitment. Basically, say what you want without being the one to ask.

You can also make it clear that with his commitment, you'll put all suitors to the side and commit solely to him. (FYI — Don't mention any "sexual" relationships, make it sound like you're referring to other men you may or may not be dating. Be elusive.)

Once you're both on the same page after your talk and you've decided you're going to allow him to have sex with you; then you need to call your hoes and inform them of the sad news you'll no longer be around. You'll need to pull the plug on any "side sex" relationships.

You shouldn't continue to have sex with anyone if you're starting to develop feelings for someone else. Just have hoes around for the times in your life when you're single and not sexually or emotionally involved with anyone. When you do get involved with someone, *even if it's emotional and not sexual*, you should probably cut the hoes off.

I personally suggest avoiding "friends with benefits" and sticking to the vibrator. You'll avoid the stress that comes along with pregnancy scares, sexually transmitted diseases, and emotional issues. If these ideas are too crazy for you, then you might be the type of woman who doesn't have a problem waiting it out. If so, be grateful, because that's one less change you'll need to make in order to beat these men at their own game.

Some women find it easy to say no and some women can never say no. We're all different and how you control yourself will vary from woman to woman. The point is to keep your legs closed and keep the pussy off limits from any man you like. It's a very easy instruction: If you like him, don't have sex with him!

It's really important as a woman, to learn to be in control of your sexual encounters. Having the "sexual upper hand" means having control over the relationship. If you're the type of woman that finds it almost impossible to say no in the heat of the moment, then you need to work on this.

Don't allow yourself to get into a situation where you can't control yourself. If you know that every time you get drunk with a man, you can't stop yourself from having sex with him, then stop drinking around men. If you're the type of woman that can't resist having sex on the first date, you MUST stop doing this.

Many women have this problem. If you're one of them, please know that you're not alone. Your inability to control yourself around men could stem from a variety of subconscious reasons such as low self-esteem, childhood trauma, abuse, loneliness, alcoholism, sexual addiction, depression… etc.

If you find yourself having difficulty with this, try your hardest to figure out why you're doing this and work hard at controlling it. If you find it virtually impossible to control, then you may have a sexual addiction. I recommend you follow up with self help books or therapy if you suspect you may have an addiction to sex.

Keep Your Sexual History a Mystery

Don't talk to men about your sex life. Ever. Never mention your sexual encounters or sexual partners. Guys don't want to hear about your buddy or that time you got drunk and had a one-night stand. They don't handle it well, at all! Remember, men don't love sluts, they don't even like them. They DO NOT like to hear about us having sex.

They get very upset and offended, *especially* if they really like you. Hearing the wrong thing about you with another man can be a turning point for a guy who does like you. He may quickly lose interest. Be careful what you say around men. Don't ever tell anyone how many partners you've had. When it comes to your past, you can be brief and uninformative. Stray far away from the details.

Men act as if they want to know, but they don't. They just don't realize they don't want to know until it's too late and they can't get the image of another man giving it to you doggy style out of their head.

If a guy is pressing you for information, you know what to do…give him the ol', "I'm a lady and I don't talk about that." These type of dumb ass lines will get you out of so much shit. He can't get mad at you for respecting yourself. He has to respect it. If he doesn't respect that answer, then you show signs of disapproval. He'll change his tone very quickly if he feels he's making you mad.

No one needs to know anything about you that you don't want them to know. It's your business. If you don't feel like sharing information, then don't!

An Important Rule You Must Follow

Do not, under any circumstance, have oral sex with

men! Yes, you read that correctly.

DO NOT HAVE ORAL SEX WITH MEN.

The second you go down on a man, you have just lost his respect. Save oral sex for the special man that earns it and deserves it. Oral sex should be even harder to get than regular sex. When you find a good man and he's everything you ever wanted, save the oral sex for him! When first dating a man, you shouldn't be having any kind of sex with him until he's earned it; especially oral sex.

If a guy's expecting oral sex, you can just tell him straight out: "I don't go down on guys. I only do that with someone I'm in a deeply committed relationship with." If a man has a problem with that, don't worry one second about it! He was just trying to use you for a blow job!

Dealing With Pressure to Have Sex

If it has only been three weeks (or even worse, just one date) and a man starts pressuring you to have sex, you can deal with his pressure with one easy statement. Basically say to him, "I'm a lady and I don't have sex with men I just met." Simple as that!

If he can't respect that, then politely tell him you're not the kind of girl he's looking for. If he starts showing signs of aggravation or anger, then flip it around! **Don't lose control! You have to be the one to get upset!**

You have to be the one that gets aggravated and says, "I have to go" or "that's messed up." Don't allow the man to be the one who's "disappointed" because he's not getting his way. **YOU** are the one that is "disappointed" in **HIM** for pressuring **YOU.**

If he doesn't stick around after that, then don't sweat it. He was just trying to screw you and he had no real interest in you. He was trying to use you for sex. You should be proud of yourself for not giving in.

You just avoided getting used. Strong, wise women do not get used. If he really likes you, he'll tell you he respects your wishes and he'll stick around. TRUST ME, when a guy likes you, he will wait for it.

Until you've found a man worthy of your affection, a good night kiss is all anyone is getting from you! You must commit to this. Giving up your precious pussy, oral sex, a hand job, or anything sexually stimulating to a man easily; without making him earn it is the **biggest mistake** you can make as a woman. You're just giving away your most precious asset for free!

When you really like a guy, things are going to start getting hot and heavy. But you know you have to keep the prize off limits. So, what do you do? There are still a few things you can do.

If it has been a few weeks and you honestly think

this guy is worthy of something; you can kiss, make out and do some touching. You may also let him get a sample by allowing access to your breasts. (Side note about breasts: Have confidence when showing your breasts to a man. Arch your back. Stick 'em out. In other words, don't be shy about your girls. Show them off. I guarantee you, he will love it.)

Make sure BEFORE things get hot and heavy that you remind him you're not willing or ready to do anything more. In addition, make sure YOU will have the strength to stop it from going further. It's easy to say you can stop yourself until you're in the moment, so be prepared.

By only allowing the man to kiss you and see your beautiful breasts, you're giving him a sample, while still maintaining the control. If he has a problem with it (which he will) simply say, "I don't like being pushed into doing more than what I want to do. I hope you can respect that." Always revert back to the "I'm a lady" excuse. It works wonders.

The guy might get frustrated when you stop him. But this is a good thing! Don't let him guilt you into anything more. Don't listen to stupid guilt trips. Simply remind him you were honest with him from the beginning. You told him already you weren't willing to do more.

If he continues to guilt you, then it's time to flip it around on him and YOU get upset. Even if you're not upset, just tell him he's upsetting you. You might have to put on a small act. Act like you're going to leave, or just act disappointed. Act as if he just ruined your night.

Tell him you're offended because he's trying to GUILT you into sex and you don't like men that do that. Tell him he's making you feel uncomfortable. **Do and say whatever is necessary to flip the guilt back to him. You must do this to retain the control.**

You should also do this because now that he's had a tiny sample, he's going to go crazy over you! If you only give a man a little piece of action, he's going to fantasize about it over and over again. You're going to be the most desirable thing to him. He won't be able to think straight. Mesmerize that man with your pussy powers.

Men Appreciate Femininity

With all this talk about vagina, it's important to remember that men love everything about women. They *crave* the pussy, but they *enjoy* all of the little things. They love the way we smell, the way we taste, the way we feel, and the way we walk. They love our breasts, butts, hips, legs, eyes, lips, thighs, and everything else. Different men love different things, but it's important to realize that it's not just your vagina they're after.

Everything about a woman is appealing to a man. On a daily basis men are constantly checking all of us out. How ironic that they're no longer stupid and unobservant when it comes to our femininity and sexuality.

Things we don't even think about are turning men on. They notice the softness of our skin, the way we look in high heels, the delicate sound of our voices, and even the way our hair smells. Men notice all of these little things and we don't even realize it.

We're the opposite of a man and that's why they're drawn to us. They are hairy and tough. We are soft and cushioned. They are tall and muscular. We are short and curvy. In their eyes, we are a work of art and they love to admire us.

Especially the men that profess to "love women". Some of them love us for our brains, talents, and all we have to offer the world. Some simply love our girlishness. For others, it's all about our shape and curves. Some men just want female companionship (because it's so loving and nurturing). Some men are just Mama's boys and need a woman in their life to take care of them.

It sounds so stupid, but it's true. Men *love* women. Embrace your femininity! Enjoy being a girl! Act like you're proud and happy to be a woman. Show men that you know the value of being a woman and watch how your world will change. Walk with confidence. Walk with your head up high, as if you know for sure you're a goddess, because to a lot of men, you are!

When you were blessed with XX chromosomes, you were given a unique gift. Being a woman is an absolute blessing. Enjoy it. Here are some ideas and tips for embracing your femininity. I derived this list from my own personal experiences of being a woman, but I also interviewed ten single men, ages 18-43. This is what we came up with together.

Please note: I'm not saying you have to do any of these things. These are just suggesions. I'm not advising that you do anything on this list, if you're not comfortable with doing it. This list was put together as a suggestion tool. You may do all of the things listed or none of the things listed. It doesn't matter as long as you have a healthy confidence in yourself (Chapter 3), your true beauty will shine through with or without these suggestions.

TIPS ON EMBRACING YOUR FEMININTY

(and other things that men love)

Nails. Get your nails done on a regular basis. Stick to a decent length, no 4-inch nails please. Look at other women of your same complexion. That will help you pick colors that look good on your shade of skin.

Toes. Do your toes to match. You don't necessarily have to go all out and get a pedicure, but at least get your toes painted the same color as your nails. When they start to chip, take the polish off! Men love French manicured toes and nails. (That seems to be a big favorite from the men interviewed.)

Shoes. Most men love a woman in heels. Designer heels will get you far with a man. Steve Madden has some of the best shoes at a decent price. You have to be careful with shoes, if it looks too unique or too outrageous, men will probably think it looks corny (that goes for everything, not just shoes). The men also said if you wear knee length boots or higher, just know you look like a whore; but a sexy whore and men love it!!!

Strut. Every man loves a woman with a sexy strut. Utilize your hips when you walk. Walk like a model, without looking like you're trying to walk like a model. Always walk confidently and comfortably. Practice your walk, if you need to. If you've never worn heels but you like the way they look and you think they're sexy, it's time to go get some heels! Don't feel embarrassed to strut your stuff, men love it. They love to watch our curves, hips, thighs and ass gracefully cross their line of sight when we walk by.

Hair. Get your hair done in a salon, unless you're good at doing your own hair. The magic a great hair stylist can do to your head is worth the money for the upkeep. Hair is a sexual stimulant to a lot of men. The men all agreed to preferring long hair (shoulder length or longer). The men interviewed said they don't mind short hair on a woman, if she has a pretty face to carry the look, but in general they are stimulated by long hair.

Make Up. The worst thing you can do with make up is over do it. If you cake on the base, stop it! You're better off wearing nothing than globbing it on. Don't over do the eye shadow. Men like it natural. Try to do your make up to where it looks natural, but it makes your features pop out. Practice putting it on, take pictures, see what you like and don't like. If you need help MAC will do your make up for $50 and teach you how to do it like a professional. Most department stores in the mall will do your make up for free, as long as you buy their products.

Fake Lashes. If you're brave enough and you really want to be a vixen, wear fake lashes. They can really make a world of difference, especially for special events. Don't buy them at the dollar store! You'll look really stupid if your eye lash starts falling off! Get them done at a licensed salon to avoid embarrassing mishaps. Stick to the short or medium lengths, as the long ones may be too much eyelash for most.

Work Out. Ugh, the dreaded dieting and exercise! It doesn't hurt to work out and eat healthy. There, I said it. If you need to shape up, just do it! I'm doing it, too. We can do it together. HOWEVER, don't let being overweight or having an out of shape body discourage you from practicing the techniques in this book. This book will work for you regardless if you are skinny, fat, or in between.

(Side note confession: I've never had a perfect body. I have always been a chunky girl. My skinniest weight was 155 lbs and I'm only five feet, four inches tall. Regardless of my little gut, flabby arms and cellulite on my thighs; I still landed a sexy, faithful, manly-man that loves me to death.

After having kids, I'm now over 200 lbs and he still considers me a sexy goddess.)

However, I won't lie to you. It doesn't hurt to look your best. Dieting and exercising is especially important if you feel bad about yourself. You see, I never felt too bad about being a bit chubby. I always embraced my figure, so I was still able to have confidence regardless of my weight. The only time being overweight will be a problem, is if it makes you unable to carry yourself with confidence.

Have you ever noticed the 400 pound women with their boyfriends? You wonder, what the hell? Well, it's because they have confidence. Their weight doesn't stop them from being sexy and confident. If you can carry yourself like that, then weight isn't an issue for you. But, if you can't then you HAVE to get yourself to a place where you're able to have that confidence, because it is absolutely necessary. (More about this in Chapter 3.)

Breasts. This is the hardest one for me to write because it is sexist and rude. However, I'm here to be honest with you and the men I interviewed all agreed on this. So, I guess I feel the need to include it. Here it is straight from the sexist horses' mouths: Men love boobs.

All of the men interviewed agreed on one thing: they love breasts. Jeez, men are such pervs. They went on to say they don't need to be perfect. Saggy and real, small and perky, or big and fake; they like them all.

Keep this in mind the next time you're intimate with a man. Remember when I said to stick those girls out with pride and confidence? They are valuable treasures to a man, so don't be afraid to show them off.

Hygiene. The things I'm going to say here should go without saying. However, the men asked me to include this information, so apparently they feel it needs to be said. If it doesn't apply to you, please don't take offense. The men said too many girls walk around like their shit doesn't stink, when in actuality, their pussy stinks. The men said it, not me! Don't shoot the messenger!

The men also encourage all women to shave "down there". They said you don't have to do the whole thing, but trim it up. Make a nice landing strip, a triangle, a patch... anything other than a huge hairy bush. Shave your arm pits. Shave your asshole. Pluck the hair out of your nipples.

If your coochie stinks, don't walk around in denial. Go to the doctor, you probably have an infection. (Hey, it's a part of being a woman, that thing needs maintenance from time to time. It's like a car. Do you want to have a shiny, new Lexus or an ugly, stinky Toyota?). Simply put, a pussy shouldn't smell bad and keep the hair under control. Random Tip: Before sex, rub a wet blow pop or some pineapple "down there" for a flavorful surprise for your man.

Observe. One thing you should ALWAYS do is take notes about what you find attractive in another woman. I know that sounds strange, but if you see something about a woman and it caught your eye, chances are it will catch a man's eyes too. It doesn't hurt to admit when another woman looks good or has great style. What is it about her that made you look? Was it her shoes, her clothes, her make-up? Figure it out and go do it for yourself. Because if it's something that caught your eye and made you admire her for a second, then it will probably catch a man's attention as well.

The point of that list wasn't to make you look like a playboy bunny, but to help you enjoy being a girl. You don't need to do any of the things listed above to practice the steps of this book. I just thought you'd like to have some concrete examples of femininity you can actually practice.

Some of you already do all of those things listed and some of you have never done any of them. Try something different. This book is marking a new chapter in your life. A time in your life when you're going to be the one in control.

A time in your life when the men are going to worship you, instead of you crying over them. A new time calls for a new look! You're becoming a new kind of woman and it isn't wrong to give yourself a new, updated look to match your new found attitude.

Not only do men appreciate women, but even women appreciate other awesome women. You may have a particular woman that you admire. What is it about her that you like? Chances are some of those qualities are already within you. Some women that I look up to are Beyonce, Rihanna, Lady Gaga, Marilyn Monroe, Coco, Fergie, and Trina.

I personally look up to these women because they are sexy and feminine, yet strong and confident. **More importantly, they do what they want to do and stand by it with firm confidence. They never back down from their choices. They don't allow men to dictate their style or personality. They are who they are and if a man doesn't like it, oh well!**

Then, after they do all that, they go out on stage in a pair of six inch heels and rock a show better than any man does. That is so sexy. These women know the value of their femininity. They know they have the power of the pussy. Study these kinds of women.

Learn how to bring out your femininity, whatever that means for YOU. Some of you might already have your look tight, but you're just not using it right. I've seen some beautiful women act like dumb fools over a man.

That's because there's more to it than just being pretty and perfect. The ugliest and fattest woman can still land a terrific man, just as a man can dog a perfect model.

Put it this way, if finding Mr. Right and living happily ever after was all about having good looks, Kim Kardashian wouldn't be on her third marriage.

We just went over a lot, and there's a lot more to learn. Let's recap everything we just learned, so we can stay on track and really sink everything in:

-A lot of men use women. They use us for sex, money, a ride, clothes, free dinners, a place to live. You name it, they're gonna drain it! If you suspect a man is using you, he probably is. Don't allow men to use you.

-Men use our emotions as leverage to get what they want.

-Control your reactions to your emotions. Especially in the beginning and in the end of relationships. You do this to maintain the upper hand and so they can no longer use your emotions against you.

-Women can prey on a man's desire for sex. (The Power of the Pussy)

-Men need us. We don't need them. Use this to your advantage.

-Flirt, but do not pursue. Be patient and let men come to you.

-Put your pussy on a pedestal. Don't give it away easily. Pretend it's a $500 bill!

-If you like him, don't have sex with him. Control yourself.

-Wait two months or more before having sex.

-Don't give men blow jobs.

-Deal with pressure to have sex by not allowing men to guilt you.

-Flip the guilt around to retain the control.

-Test your man with the Prince Charming Test before allowing him to have sex with you.

-Use PEAK to your fullest advantage!!!

-Don't be afraid to ask for what you want, but be prepared to walk away if he won't give it to you.

-Enjoy being a girl. Embrace your femininity.

Chapter 3

THE POWER OF CONFIDENCE

If you learn nothing else in this book, please remember these first three chapters. They are laying the foundation necessary to change your mentality about men. Once you change your mental beliefs about men and dating, you will be able to change your outcomes with men. This all lies within you being able to control your reaction to your emotions, using the power of your pussy, all while projecting and maintaining a strong confidence in yourself.

Confidence is king. The only way you can begin to deal with men is through *sheer confidence*. If you love yourself and you value yourself, the men in your life will too. If you know in your heart you are a wonderful woman, worthy of getting everything you deserve, then you will get just that.

If you don't value yourself, you will always end up with the men at the bottom of the barrel. You receive what you believe! If you believe you're shit, you will get shit. If you believe you deserve the best, you will get the best. So, I don't care if you're the ugliest piece of shit walking the Earth. You need to walk with your head up high and tell yourself you're beautiful. Even if you don't believe it, fake it!

Look at this way: Low self-esteem is a waste of energy. Whether you have low self-esteem or not, you're still the same person with the same flaws. There's nothing you can do about it. Why waste time feeling bad about it? Feeling bad about yourself isn't going to make you look any better. You're just wasting precious energy on unproductive, negative thoughts. Just accept yourself for who you are, embrace it, and move forward.

For a person with low self-esteem, this may be the hardest thing to change. It's not easy getting over a bad self-image, but it is a *necessity* if you want your love life to change. In all honesty, you MUST get a grip on your self-esteem. Not only will it help your interactions with men, but your overall happiness will improve.

For one month, I want you to walk around with a healthy self-esteem and see what happens. Pretend you like yourself. Even better, pretend you LOVE YOURSELF. Just pretend, be an actress. You'll be amazed at how much happier you become.

Self-Esteem and Culture

I used to have low self-esteem. VERY low self-esteem. I was a young white American girl, living in the suburban world. This meant I was never skinny enough and my breasts were never big enough. I had too much cellulite. My skin was too pale. I wasn't tall enough. I wasn't pretty enough. The list of imperfections could go on and on. Simply put, I felt ugly. I was depressed about the way I looked. I had a classic case of low self-esteem.

Then, in the beginning of 10th grade, I went to live with my Mom in Miami. I was sent to finish high school at Edison Senior High; an all black school located in the heart of Little Haiti. Now, when I say an all black school, I was literally one of three white people in my entire high school.

It wasn't an easy experience, as anyone who has ever been a minority can attest to the difficulties of adapting to the majority. However, it was a life-changing experience, and I wouldn't change it regardless of how difficult it was at times. I learned so much from my experiences at this school. One of the greatest lessons I learned was about self-esteem, self-image, and self-worth. Why? What does this cultural experience have to do with self-esteem?

The reason is because suburban culture is cruel and urban culture just does not give a fuck what anyone thinks! We don't even realize it's happening, but suburban culture (which is my politically correct way of saying "white" culture) has a nasty way of telling you: "You're ugly. Look at all the things wrong with you! You're ten pounds overweight, fatty. Your hair is frizzy. You're too short. Your nose is too pointy. You have cellulite and by the way, if you haven't noticed, your boobs are too small!?!?!"

Urban culture (which is my politically correct way of saying "black" culture) says, "Fuck you and your opinions. I am who I am. I may not be perfect, but I'm fine the way I am. Anyone that has a problem with the way I look can just look the other way."

I was in awe of my fellow peers. Their perceptions of themselves were always positive. Of course, there was still teasing and bullying within the school, but it just didn't matter. It was a complete awakening. You mean we don't have to cower down to bashing ourselves and each others' imperfections at every opportunity? We can reject it? What a relief! What liberation!

You see, before my transfer to this school, all I saw was everything wrong with myself. In my mind, every imperfection I had was magnified. Then, I go to this school and the shift in perception was a huge awakening.

I came to realize the way I perceived myself was a figment of my own imagination, which was over-developed from years of outside influences. (Magazines, kids at school, make up commercials, music videos, etc...) All of these people and things were making me feel shitty about myself, but the problem wasn't the outside sources.

The problem was me!

I was ***allowing*** them to make me feel that way! It was my *choice* to believe it, as much as it was my *choice* to reject it. The number one difference between people that get depressed over the way they look and the ones who embrace the way they look, is that people with low self-esteem **CHOOSE** to allow people to bring them down.

You can **CHOOSE** to let it bother you...

or you can **CHOOSE** to tell them to fuck off!

The day I told the world to fuck off was the day I was able to take the blinders off and see myself for who I was... an imperfectly beautiful person. My imperfections make me who I am. Who I am is an awesome human being, because there's no one like me in the world.

Now outsiders can either accept me for who I am or not. If they don't, that's okay. That's their loss. It's no longer my problem. **The greatest part about gaining confidence is the tremendous relief you feel after becoming free of people's opinions.**

Now that I'm out of school and have gone on with my life, I took my lessons with me. I know I'm beautiful, and if one guy doesn't think so, he can keep moving because another one will! *Everyone has flaws.* Don't let anyone make you feel bad about your imperfections. They aren't perfect, either!

Don't sit around and allow one person's perception of you define who you are. This is exactly what some girls do. They'll hang on to the one guy that tells her she's ugly, stupid, or fat, and take his opinion as the ultimate truth! This is a tactic used by insecure men, so be careful.

Insecure Men

His goal is to make her feel so bad about herself that she eventually believes no other man will want her. Are you in a situation like this? If so, just know this guy is using your emotions and lack of confidence against you.

He's not saying these things because they're true. If they were true, why would he be with you?! He's saying these mean things as a way to keep you down. If he keeps you down, he keeps you around. This stems from his own insecurity.

A secure man tells his woman she's beautiful because he's sure she will never leave him. This is because he knows he's a great man and doesn't need to fear other men stealing his woman. An insecure man has to put his woman down because he fears losing her to a better man. His insurance against this loss is to put her down so much, that she becomes paralyzed by insecurities. Be aware of this tactic and don't ever fall into believing some asshole's negative opinion of you.

Confidence is So Sexy

Nothing can make a person more attractive than sheer confidence. Knowing who they are and embracing it. Being sure about who they are and never backing down from it. When a person is confident, they're able to relax and be themselves around others. This makes the people around them happy, relaxed, and comfortable too. Confidence has nothing to do with your looks or body. *It has everything to do with being you and not apologizing for it.*

For example, there are some physically unattractive people who are considered very sexy people. They have something special within. They know it and they embrace it. I'm sure you've had a crush on a guy who wasn't a perfect ten, but something about him turned you on.

These kinds of people have confidence and self worth. Wrap that together with what they have to offer (next section) and it makes them undeniably sexy. Here are some examples of people who aren't the stereotypical definitions of what sexy is, but ironically, they are labeled sexy by someone:

Sarah Jessica Parker

Jay-Z

Eminem

Madonna

Angelina Jolie

Christopher Walken

Dog the Bounty Hunter

Lil' Wayne

Barbara Streisand

50 Cent

Fergie

Fred Durst

Miley Cyrus

Billy Bob Thornton

Lady Gaga

Kid Rock

You may not find some of these people attractive, but to someone out there, they're the sexiest person alive. Angelina Jolie is a perfect example. Some people find her to be the most beautiful woman alive, while other people don't understand why.

Think about this: Madonna has a huge gap in her teeth and she was the number one sex symbol of the eighties. Lil' Wayne would be considered short and ugly to most people, but there's thousands of women that think he is the sexiest guy in the world. Fergie's face looks worn out and tired, but she's absolutely gorgeous. Jay-Z is definitely not the definition of a good-looking man, but he managed to marry one of the most beautiful women on the planet!

The people on that list have one thing in common: confidence. They know who they are. They know what they have to offer. They know they are unique in their talents and they embrace their individuality. It is indeed their persona, backed by their sureness in themselves, which allows sexiness to exude off them. When a person does not like them for whatever reason, they don't care!

If someone points out their flaws, they don't obsess over it. Famous people are being criticized all day, every day in magazines, on TV, and online. If they paid attention and believed just a fraction of all the bashing and hateful things they hear, they wouldn't want to get out of bed in the morning. They wouldn't be able to do anything. They'd become paralyzed by the fear of what others were thinking. They don't have time to care what people think.

They *choose* not to care what people think.

They also don't go around pointing out all of the things wrong with them. Who wants to hear that? No one cares if 50 Cent hates his buckteeth and bullet scars. No one cares if Eminem thinks his nose is pointy and long. No one cares if you think you're FAT! No one cares if you think you're UGLY! You're the only one worried about it. If someone does worry about it, then they can fuck off.

The Message Low Self-Esteem Sends to Men

Showing low self-esteem is a sure way to send a bad message to a man. When you put yourself down in front of a man, not only is he turned off, but it's annoying. Even worse, to a person who preys on women, it's a sign that you can be used! Please remember this. When you down yourself in front of a man who knows how to play women, you're wearing a big sign on your forehead that says:

-I'm an easy target.

-I will be easy to use.

-I'm going to be easy to get into bed, because I don't value myself.

-I don't realize what I have, therefore I will give it away easily.

-You can play me and I won't mind.

-I'll forgive you easily because I don't think I'm worthy of respect.

I'm sure you never realized you were sending these messages, but this is *exactly* what you're saying to men who use women. Now, for the men who don't use women, your low self-esteem is simply turning them off. Downing yourself, complaining about yourself, and pointing out your flaws is ugly and unattractive to men. Stop it!

We're so caught up in our flaws to the point that we're talking about them, touching them, squeezing them, and covering them. All in an attempt to conceal them from the world, but ironically, we end up pointing them out!

For example, I have a slight overbite and anytime I would laugh, I'd cover my mouth. Then people would always ask me, why do you cover your mouth when you laugh? I'd respond, "I hate my teeth." In my efforts to conceal my overbite, all I did was call attention to it. And, even worse, call attention to my low self esteem.

Once I got my confidence, I stopped doing that. Now, I smile proud. Now, guess what people tell me? They tell me I have a pretty smile! I was perplexed. Are these people being cruel and teasing me? Are they serious?

Then my husband told me one day that my overbite was cute. He went on to tell me it was a unique feature and it's something he's always LIKED about me. Don't hide what makes you unique. Let it shine... because you never know who's looking and enjoying what they see.

What we fail to realize is that most men don't even focus on the things wrong with us. They don't even notice these stupid little things. All they see is this beautiful, feminine being. Then here you go, pointing out everything wrong with yourself and then they start to see it. Then they probably start to second-guess why they're attracted to you.

In reality, most men are simply thinking: "Boobs. Ass. Curves. Hair smells good. Yum. I want some of that." (Yes, men think like this as they look at you.) They don't look at you and think, "Wow, her nose is big and her teeth are crooked. She must be about 20 pounds overweight."

They don't do that. We do that. Women are the overly critical ones. We notice all of the little things wrong with men and with ourselves. Therefore, I guess it's natural for us to assume men are doing the same type of nit picking, but they're not.

Another way to think about the power of confidence is that you are your biggest salesperson. If a car salesman is trying to sell you a car but all he's doing is talking about what's wrong with the car and never mentions anything good about it, would you buy the car? No. You probably wouldn't even waste your time test-driving it! If no one is buying your "car," could it possibly be that you've been a shitty saleswoman?

Here are some tips on how to stop downing yourself:

-Don't mention anything negative about yourself to anyone EVER.

-Look in the mirror and tell yourself you're beautiful. (Even if you don't think you are, just do it every day until you at least become comfortable with your image.)

-Compare yourself to someone uglier than you, and then give thanks that you're prettier than that person is. (I know that's mean, but sometimes you need to change your perspective.)

-Don't point out your flaws. Not even to yourself. Just ignore the things you hate, rather than staring at them in the mirror all day!

-Don't say stupid, annoying things like: "I hate myself," or the classic, "I'm so fat." Especially if you weigh 125 lbs! Nothing annoys men more than the skinny girl that constantly complains about how fat she is.

-Never call yourself stupid.

-Make a list of all the good things you have and from now on only point out these things.

-When you feel bad about yourself, take out the list of good things and read it.

Confidence Doesn't Mean Conceit

Now, some of you are on another level. You don't have low self-esteem, you have an overly confident self-esteem and this is bad too. The two types of women that men stray away from are women who put themselves down and women that are conceited.

The trick is to have a fine balance. Confidence is that fine balance. Confidence is not to be confused with arrogance. It's important we know the difference. Here are some things a conceited woman may do and some of the challenges she may face due to her overgrown ego:

The Conceited Woman

-She will only talk to the "perfect" guys, ignoring all of the others. She may even go as far as being rude or cruel to men she feels are "beneath" her. This only limits her choices and makes finding a good man an impossible task. Plus, it's rude and uncalled for. Don't be mean to a man for approaching you. It took him a lot of courage, give him that much respect and dismiss him politely.

-She looks in the mirror and thinks she looks better than other women do.

-She makes fun of other women or always notices negative things in other people.

-Pretends to be perfect, but deep inside she uses the conceit as a mask for low self-esteem or even worse, self-hatred.

-She usually ends up hurt in her relationships because she's always looking for a "perfect" mate. We all know there is no such thing, but she keeps striving for perfection, only to end up disappointed.

-She refuses to grasp the concept that no one is perfect, not even her. Therefore, she usually ends up with an equally conceited "perfect" person who probably puts her down or hurts her, because he himself can't grasp that no one is perfect.

-While this couple may look great and "perfect" on the

outside, behind closed doors there are big problems. There will be egos clashing, periodical insults, control issues and/or jealousy.

-Whether it comes from the male, the female or both; one person will always be the better one and the other will be left feeling inferior.

-She'll push away a lot of men, because conceit is a TURN OFF.

Now here are some examples of the confident woman, so you can see the difference.

The Confident Woman

-Gives a man respect, even if she isn't interested in him. She won't make him feel bad for attempting to approach her. She'll dismiss him in a polite manner.

-She looks in the mirror and sees a beautiful woman.

-Compliments other women, sees the beauty in other women because she doesn't feel threatened by them.

-Gives a man an initial chance, even if he isn't the finest guy in the room because she isn't vain. Therefore, she isn't pushing away potentially good men and limiting her choices.

-Knows she isn't perfect, so she doesn't expect perfection from a mate.

-Still has self-doubt and things she dislikes about herself, but feels good about herself regardless of her flaws.

-She'll have healthier relationships with men because she is accepting of her own faults; then she can be accepting of a mate's faults.

-Will stay away from conceited men or men with low self-esteem.

-Will attract more men because self-confidence is a TURN ON.

Now you can see why it's so important to learn confidence; but not to over exaggerate and become conceited. Think about these differences in men. If a man is confident, it's sexy. However, if he's cocky and conceited, it makes you want to run the other way. Even if he's the finest person in the world, he doesn't need to be an arrogant dick about it.

His conceit turns you off and makes him unattractive. The same goes for women. *Beauty comes more from the inside than it does the outside. The prettiest person in the world can ruin their beauty by having an ugly inside.*

The level of confidence you have in yourself comes out on so many levels. People can see how you view yourself not only by the things you say about yourself, but by the way you walk, the way you talk, and the way you act. Confidence can be heard verbally, seen physically, and felt emotionally.

Be careful. That negativity in your mind is flowing out of you on every level. Just as confidence flows out of you on all of those levels. The people around you can feel and see your confidence. It is a HUGE part of who you are.

If you know that you are going to have issues in this area, I suggest that you commit to doing whatever is necessary to conquer this demon. Even if you need to go to counseling to gain a healthy, self image. Whatever it takes for you to establish a sure confidence in yourself is what you need to do.

Some women will find this chapter not to be an issue, while others may struggle to ditch the self-hating, self-bashing mind set. If you cannot seem to move past negative thoughts about yourself or you are struggling to get to a place where you are 100% confident, I am sad to say that you're never going to be able change your outcomes with men.

However, there is a light at the end of the tunnel. You do not have to live your life looking down on yourself. If you work at improving this you will get better, I promise. Once you get to a place where you are perfectly content and happy with yourself you will feel so liberated!

Confidence is a glorious thing!

The Offerings

Everyone has a reason to be confident because everyone has something to offer. That's why I said, "I don't care if you're the ugliest piece of shit walking the planet," because it really isn't about looks. It's about what you have to "offer."

What you have to offer are your talents, personality, hobbies, accomplishments, and so on. They are the special things about you that make you who you are and make you different from others around you.

That's why the people on that list of famous people can be confident even though they might not be "perfect tens." They have something to offer the world in their talents, they know it, and that's what they focus on. That doesn't mean they don't notice their imperfections. They just choose to focus on the good and forget about the bad.

Every person has multiple things to offer. They vary from person to person. I have stuff to offer which makes me valuable, and it's different from what you have to offer, which makes you valuable. You need to figure out what you have to offer. Here are examples of things worthy of admiration, which do not pertain to looks:

-A career or great job

-You're a kick ass Mom

-Educated or going to school.

-Have a car.

-You have your own place.

-You're a very loving and compassionate person

-Great cook

-Keep a clean house

-Funny or fun to be around

-You go to church

-You're from a great family

-You're faithful, you never cheat on a mate

-You have great friends

This list could go on and on, but at least you have some ideas. You might not think these are things worthy of value. You may think they're stupid and don't matter. Now ask yourself, when a guy has these things, aren't they pluses in your book? So, why shouldn't they be valued in you?

You think little things like that don't matter to men, but they do. Look at it this way, have you ever liked a person who wasn't the finest person in the world; but he had a job, a car, and he was a lot of fun? You really liked him a lot and so you overlooked the fact he had little imperfections. It was his personality and offerings that made you like him.

We are initially drawn to people because of physical attraction, but we stay around when we become attracted to who they are and what they have to offer.

Make a list in your journal of at least ten things you have to offer, even more if you can get them down, but at least ten. These attributes can't be physical or sexual. Don't write down, "I have a nice ass" or "I'm sexy." These have to be personality traits, talents, goals, achievements, etc… (Hey, a car is an achievement; don't be afraid to be proud of it, even if it is an old clunker!). Here is my list:

-Educated

-Funny

-I can cook

-I'm a great mother / very loving

-I love to dance

-I'm faithful

-I own my own business

-I'm very spiritual

-I have my own car

-I'm honest

-I'm bilingual

-I have a great extended family

Any man would be lucky to have me! This is what you have to do. Right now. Go make your list and write at the bottom of it in big letters: "Any man would be lucky to have me!"

Visit the list when you get down on yourself. Once you know who you are and what you have to offer, never forget. Use these qualities to help boost your self-esteem. These qualities are worthy parts of YOU. Remember, you would admire and enjoy these same qualities if they were in a man you were dating.

Chapter 4

THE POWER OF BEING THE GAME

What's the Game?

Now we're getting to the fun! When you have a healthy self-esteem and you know what you have to offer, you begin to see your true self worth. You are a wonderful person and you're worthy of nothing less than an equally wonderful man. You won't settle for anything less because you are *so worth it*. Plus, you have a vagina! Why should you settle for less?

You shouldn't! You should **NEVER** settle for less. From now on, you're going to walk around thinking, "I'm special and any man would be lucky to have me." If you don't believe it, say it to yourself everyday until you do. You can start out pretending, but eventually you'll have to truly believe it.

You have to get a bit of a selfish attitude. Any man who eventually lands you, has won a prize. You're that fucking special. Truly, in all honesty, you are that special. There is no one in the world like you. You are the only one.

Your life experiences, personality, culture, looks, accomplishments, sense of humor... everything about you is unique. Since you are so unique and special, any man interested in you must work hard and prove he's worthy of your attention and time. He literally has to "win" you.

From this moment forward you are to look at yourself

as if you are a prize to be won.

You'll have many men playing and competing in this game — the game of "winning your love." Only the best man will win the game. He'll have to do everything right in order to win. Everything you want him to do.

What's the Prize?

Contestants will receive your attention and time, but only the winner will receive your love and respect. You know how to control your emotions and you know not to rush in to developing feelings for a man too quickly. Now you'll easily be able to stop giving out love and affection to unworthy men. Once you know he's an absolute winner, then you can allow him to get close to your heart.

So, what do you want him to do? Think about this. What type of requirements will a man need in order to be a contestant? Better yet, what will it take for contestants to win?

Write down ten things you really want in a man. When making the list, really think about your dream man. If you could design your perfect guy, what type of qualities would he have? These ten things should be exactly what you require from a man **before** you allow your emotions to come into the picture. Be reasonable. Don't make it so outrageous that no man will ever be able to meet your list. You can list physical attributes, as well. Some reasonable requests are:

- ✓-Honest
- ✓-Dependable
- ✓-Good Looking
- ✓ -Educated
- ✓ -Tall
- ✓ -Generous
- ✓-Good Sense of Humor
- ✓ -Has a job
- ✓-Has a car
- ✓-Has his own place
- ✓ -Nice body
- ✓-Kind
- -Would make a good Father

These qualities could be a number of things and it will vary from woman to woman. For instance, if you're 18, you might not expect the person you're looking for to have his own place; but if you're 35, that better be on your list!

Perhaps you might be a woman that is lied to a lot by men. Therefore, you better put honesty as a top priority. Every woman desires different things from a man. Some of you might only date tall guys, while others don't care about height. This list is all about what YOU want.

You might come up with 25 things, but narrow it down to the top ten. This way you know what's really important to you. Once you've determined what you really want, it'll be easy to sift through the losers and the winners of the "who will win your love" game.

If a man doesn't meet a majority of your requirements, especially the important ones, *let him go!!!* Even if you like the guy a lot. I know this may be hard to do, but *remember to control your emotions*. If he can't meet at least half of your requirements, then he isn't even worthy of playing the game. This means, he's not even on your radar! Forget about him. Scratch him off the list and move on to the next one. Don't waste time on anyone who isn't worth it.

The reason you need to have high standards and put yourself on a pedestal is because men enjoy the chase. They like the game. They WANT to play the "who can win her love" game. They love the thrill of the hunt. Remember that. As much as you may hate the bullshit games, it's the reality of a man's mentality. This is literally the process of courting a woman. They want to court. Let them court.

When you make it hard for a man to get close to you, you become a pussy challenge. There is nothing a man loves more than a pussy challenge! When you have confidence, you don't have an issue making a man put forth effort to get your time and attention. This makes you one of those women that are hard to get. Now, men will see you as a thrilling challenge instead of an easy target, booty call, or a girl desperate for love and attention.

They now see a mature woman who knows what she wants, knows what she's worth and is looking for a good man. She's going to require her potential suitors to step up. They're now prepared to either play the game or walk away.

If they walk away, then they weren't looking for love, just sex. The ones that stick it out and play the game are genuinely interested in you. Let the game begin. Who will win? Now that part is all up to you, instead of the other way around. Congratulations, you are in control!

Remember, only fools rush in. If you have been giving up your love, heart, sex or emotion too easily; then you've been making it way too easy for men. That's why they lose interest. They can easily win the game. They have no reason to stick around. They have no reason to be honest, faithful, kind, compassionate or thoughtful. They won the game and they're on to a new challenge. Failure to accept this fact will leave you hurt by men again and again.

The day you make it hard and make them fight for your affection is the day they'll begin to pursue you, respect you, chase after you and wait patiently for your love. Not all men will, but you already know why, it's because he's not genuinely interested in you. Don't take it personally, forget about him and move onto the next man.

Men are like buses. Miss one and in 15 minutes

another one's coming. Plus, later in the book, I'll show you how to have men lining up to date you. So don't worry about where to find all of these potential suitors.

Enjoy Kicking Losers to The Curb, It's Fun!

Be prepared to kick men to the curb. It's going to happen... a lot! You aren't going to come across your dream guy on the first or second time around. But, if you're impatient and settle for the first or second guy to come your way, then you'll never find your real winner.

The reality is you have to sift through A LOT of losers to get to that winner. I probably dated (I said dated, not fucked, don't get it confused!) 20 different guys over the course of three years before I met my future husband. Had I settled with the first one to make me smile, I would have never met the man of my dreams. So, enjoy kicking the losers to the curb. It doesn't have to be a grueling and depressing process. It's all a big game. So, have fun.

How We Ruin Our Own Game

One mistake, he loses the game and it's time for the next player to get a chance! *This is where so many of us screw up*. We get hung up on one guy. We get tunnel vision. We focus in on him and all of a sudden our attention is completely distracted.

THIS IS ALL WRONG! We have to stop doing this. **When you're single you should ALWAYS have two, three, or even four guys that you are seeing at one time.** These aren't boyfriends or men you're having sex with. These are just guys you're dating. If you're a single woman, you have the right to date whomever you want and you should!

I strongly encourage all single women to have *at least* two potential men you're dating at one time. It's very important for several reasons: Having multiple men in your life keeps you from getting hung up on one man. It will also give you strength to move on, if the man you like a lot is not reciprocating the same feelings.

In addition, this will help you with the power of keeping yourself busy (Chapter 8). It also gives you confidence and strength when dealing with men because you always have back ups! Besides, the "who can win her love game" won't be very fun if there aren't a lot of players!

Men Are Like Pots On a Stove

How Many Pots Can You Cook At One Time?

From now on I want you to look at the men in your life as pots cooking on a stove. You have four burners. That's four slots for four men. (If you can't handle four at one time right now, then pretend your stove has 2 or 3 slots). If you're dating different guys, you're going to have men you like a lot and men you don't like very much.

They're not all going to be sexy heart throbs. You're going to have a few frogs in there, too. So, the guys you like a lot go on the front burners and get the most attention. The frogs you don't like so much stay on the back burners, and get less attention. But, they're there when you need them.

So, if at any time your good guys on the front burners start acting up or pissing you off, you throw 'em to the back burner and move another guy into his slot. Or, throw him away all together and replace him with a back burner guy or a completely new man! It may be hard for you to get the hang of dealing with multiple men at one time. Trust me, it takes some skill. Names get confused, men get their feelings hurt, and it can get overwhelming.

Start off with dating two men at one time. Then move to three or four. They don't all have to be potential boyfriend material. You could have one guy you're dating, one is a sugar daddy, and the other one is your fuck buddy. You could have two filler dates and two guys you really like. Whatever combination or variety you choose, is completely up to you. See how many you can handle at one time. It's fun!

Men do the same thing to us. Don't feel bad about this. If you're single, you have the right to see whoever you want! You don't owe anyone anything. As long as you're being honest and you're not committed to anyone (cheating), then why should you feel bad about dating multiple men? You shouldn't...

Don't ever let the men know, of course! Be elusive. They don't need to know anything. If the subject comes up, just say, "I'm a single woman and I'm enjoying my freedom. I'm dating and not really looking for a relationship at the moment." Leave it at that. Don't elaborate. Remember, men hate hearing about us with other men.

On the other hand, if one of your "back burner" men starts pressuring you into a relationship, you can say, "I told you I was enjoying being single and not looking for a relationship." This is the fun part of being single. Enjoy turning men down. Enjoy being picky.

There are so many men in this world. Enjoy the fun of dating them all! More importantly, remember not to get hung up on one guy. The minute you do, you will fuck everything up. Be careful...

Don't waste your time on losers, users, or abusers. Don't sit around waiting for Mr. Perfect to magically appear. Stop waiting for your current Mr. Asshole to turn into Mr. Perfect. It's never going to happen!

Get out there and start having FUN. *Stop taking dating so seriously. It's just a game. Games are meant to be fun.* Start meeting and getting to know different men. Don't be afraid to have fun dating different men and then dropping them when they aren't what you want. Men do it to us all the time!!! They don't feel any guilt about, so why should we?

You are only young and single once, so you should enjoy this time in your life. One day you will find Mr. Right, get married, and settle down into a lifelong commitment. You'll look back and wish you had enjoyed your single years. So, stop worrying so much about finding Mr. Right and have fun with all of the Mr. Right Nows. Because when you're not looking for love, is when it likes to come plop down into your lap.

Don't Forget Variety

Date a variety of men. If you only date young guys, date an older guy for a change. If you always date thugs; then try going out with a clean cut, preppy guy. If you normally date white collar guys, try out a blue collar guy. Have one of each. Enjoy yourself!

Chapter 5

THE POWER OF TAKING OUT THE TRASH

This chapter is going to address the women who are currently in bad relationships or who may be having a hard time getting over a relationship. There are 3.5 *BILLION* men on the planet. In America alone, there are more than 18 million single men. Why would you waste your precious time on the one man who is unwilling to love and respect you the way you want? There are so many other men left out there.

Why do we do this? We get with a guy who is an absolute loser or treats us badly; but because we "love" him, we try to fix all of his problems. We ignore all of his faults and then try to mold him into the type of man we really want. We try to rescue and save them, even when they don't want to be saved!

Why? Why? Why? I believe it goes back to being natural nurturers combined with having low self-esteem. Although the woman doing it will tell you it's because, "I love him." That's bullshit! You can love many men in your lifetime.

Just because you picked this one guy out of the billions of men out there as "the one," does that mean you should give all your time and effort to him? I'm sorry, but "I love him" isn't a good enough reason to stay with a man who isn't treating you well. It's time to stop using that emotional crutch to stand by a man that's not worthy of you. It's time to take out the trash.

If you don't get rid of the trash NOW, I'm going to tell you what's going to happen: You're going to spend the next few years of your life focusing on "fixing" a guy who can't be fixed. Then, while you're busy rescuing a loser from his own stupidity, a thousand great guys have come and gone. *You just missed out on all the good men, because you're focusing on this one guy.* Before you know it, years have passed and your man is still not fixed. He's still a jerk, a cheater, a liar, a loser, or whatever he is; and worst of all, he's still treating you badly!

This "fix" him crap is a big waste of your time and energy. Stop wasting your efforts. Assholes will always be assholes. Cheaters will always be cheaters. Users will always be users. Since the beginning of time, women have tried to change men and it has rarely ever worked to the woman's advantage. It usually leaves the woman drained and hurt.

You should also keep in mind that you'll only be young and beautiful for so long. Don't waste your youth trying to help your man. *Help yourself.* If you need to fix someone, fix yourself. Don't waste this precious time in your life focused on someone who isn't worthy or appreciative of your time, let alone your love.

Don't get me wrong. If you have a good man and you're working together toward a common goal, help your man. Is he working while you go to school or vice versa? Then stand by his side. However, chances are you don't have a good man working with you or else you wouldn't have purchased this book. Chances are you're the one putting forth all of the effort in your relationship, while he's getting a free pass or barely helping out.

How to Know When It's Time to Leave Your Man

Do you know how to tell when you're dating a man who is waste of your time? When your parents don't like him. It's that easy. Or, your friends don't like him. Possibly, you can't even bring him around your parents or friends. If that's the case, there is definitely something wrong with him!

You have to ask yourself, why would they lie? What do they have to gain from lying to you? Nothing. Your parents only want what's best for you. If they see a guy hanging around their daughter and he's not doing right by her, they aren't going to like him. It doesn't matter that they don't know him the way you do. It doesn't matter if they "misunderstand" him.

Don't try to make excuses for your man: "Oh, my Dad doesn't like him because of that one time...." Blah! Blah! Blah! The people around you can clearly see what kind of guy he is. It will take awhile for you to realize it because you have emotional blinders on. Even though you know deep down inside that this guy isn't the right guy for you.

You are in denial. You know you aren't being treated right, but you hang around. This is because either you're obsessed with fixing him, winning him over, or you're hoping and waiting for him to change. You could just be obsessed with being "in love." You think that because you "love" him, you should stick it out.

Maybe you just don't want to admit you were wrong, so you hold on to the guy. How much longer will you wait? How many more years of your life will you waste? What will it take? The people in your life that truly love you can easily see when someone isn't right for you. They don't have on those emotional blinders. They can see right through him.

You can't see as clearly as someone who's standing on the outside, looking in. That's why you should always listen to your parents and friends. If all of your friends dislike the guy, that's a sure sign for you to move on. If your family hates the guy with a passion, it's time to move on.

Do You Enjoy Being Sad?

I know it hurts to admit the guy you love is no good. It's hard to throw away all of the time you've invested into this man. It's not going to be easy. You really do love him, and I believe you. But, love is not enough! Is loving him worth the pain?

Do you *enjoy* being sad? Do you *enjoy* crying? Do you *enjoy* wondering where he is or why he isn't picking up the phone? No. You're making yourself miserable and love isn't a good enough excuse to be miserable.

There are two reasons beyond our inability to control our emotions, and beyond our low self-esteem as to why we put up with crap from men. Number one, we want immediate gratification. We'll get with an unfaithful man or an asshole just because he's a good looking guy and gets the blood pumping. Then we want to play the "who can win his heart" game. We want to play and we want to win! All for that satisfying gratification.

The second reason is we don't want to be single. We hate being single! We hate it because it's a lonely world and because it has this social stigma that something is wrong with you. We're so eager not to be single that we refuse to wait and be patient for Mr. Right. Instead of waiting it out for a good man, we settle for a mediocre man. We hate being lonely so much that we would rather take crap than be alone.

You have probably ended up stuck in this rut. You're single and you want to find a man, so you take the first cute guy to come around, or the first guy to give you some attention. You ignore all of the signs warning you he's a loser. Therefore, you unintentionally settle for less, and it isn't until you have your heart invested that you really start to reconsider. But, by this time, it's too late, because you "love" him now. You're stuck.

From this moment forward, you're no longer settling for less. Here are some signs to help you identify a loser, whether you're dating one now or to avoid one in the future. If your guy is showing any of these signs, you need to walk away now! Don't invest anymore time and feelings into a man displaying any of the following signs:

How to Spot a Loser

-You catch him lying about where he was or who he was with.

-You catch him cheating, even if it wasn't sex. Even "talking" with another girl inappropriately is cheating. He knows it's wrong, but he doesn't care. Ask yourself, if he caught you doing the same thing, would he be upset? If so, it's cheating.

-He doesn't have anything to offer. He doesn't have a car, a job, he's not in school, or he's a grown ass man that lives with his mom. He shows no signs of ever growing up and being responsible.

-He has three kids with three different women…you better run away fast, or you'll be next!

-He doesn't take care of his kids the way a man should. (Don't make excuses for him.)

-He never buys you anything. Not even flowers on your birthday or a present at Christmas time. Or, if he does buy you something, it's a cheap piece of shit that he bought out of guilt or because you told him he'd better buy you something.

-He's in and out of jail, repeatedly. Give it up....

-He's a drug addict. Has he stolen money from your purse?

(*A note about drug addicts: don't pity your addicted mate. Addiction is a cruel disease, but it can be overcome. If you require him to be drug free and he can't or won't stop, you need to move on. Love *is* enough to lead someone to recovery. If he's unwilling to change, then you must counter-act by being unwilling to love.)

-He has no future, no ambition, or no drive to succeed.

-He treats you badly or is disrespectful to you.

-He doesn't label you as his girlfriend or he lies to people about the status of your relationship. When a man loves a woman, he wants to show her off, not hide her.

-He doesn't bring you around his friends or he treats you like shit in front of them.

-He doesn't bring you around his family or treats you like shit in front of them.

How to Spot a User

Another type of trash you need to be aware of is the user. The user is the worst because he **knows** what he's doing. If you're dating a person who has NOTHING to offer, the type of person that brings NOTHING to the table, if you find yourself doing all of the work in the relationship...you are being used.

He's playing you like a fiddle. He makes you think

he really loves you and cares about you but his actions speak for his true nature. He says he loves you and then asks to borrow your car. He says he wants to marry you, and then asks to borrow some cash he never repays.

Whatever his style is...you can sense when you're being used. Your intuition tells you loud and clear but you block it out. You don't want to believe the guy you love is nothing but a user, pimping your ass. It happens all the time, so be careful!

Just as men need to look out for gold diggers, women need to be on the look out for users. *There are a lot more of them than you may think.* Unlike a gold digger looking for big bucks, most men that use women are satisfied with way less. You don't have to have a lot of money to get used by a man. You just need to be naïve.

Users don't just use women for money or sex. They'll use you for a place to live. They'll use you so they don't have to work. Users are not only guys you just started dating, they could be your husband.

It doesn't matter if you've been together for two weeks or twelve years. A user is a user. The longer he's been with you just means you were easy to use, and he's gotten comfortable. Hey, if someone else is willing to do all the work, why wouldn't a guy stick around?

This isn't putting down men who stay at home with the kids. I don't think they're users. Some people might not agree with it, but I don't think there's anything wrong with a man staying home with the kids and tending to the household duties while the woman works.

IF! Things are 50/50! If you go to work and he stays home with the kids, but when you get home you have to cook dinner and wash laundry; that's not 50/50. You should each get equal amounts of time to relax and equal amounts of work and effort put in.

Users come in all different forms. The man using you for sex. The one using you for a place to live. The guy using you to buy him clothes, gifts, or take him out to eat. The unemployed husband using you for fifteen years.

They are everywhere and they come in all different packages. Here are some ways to tell if you're being used. Is your man doing any of the things below? If so, chances are you are being used.

-You're the only one working or you're the only one that ever has any money. When he does have money, he never spends it on you or with you. He seems to have more important things to do.

-You pay for dinner and everything else…

-He always asks to borrow your car.

-You take care of the house, the kids, and work a 40-hour work week while he just hangs out.

-He asks to borrow money. Even if he pays you back. He is

just getting you comfortable for the next time, when he asks for a bigger amount...which he won't pay back. Beware of this tactic.

-He doesn't have anything to offer. No car, no job, no home...nothing at all to offer.

-He tells you he loves you, but he never shows it. Warning: You're just an ATM machine to him. He has to say, "I love you" to get the cash. "I love you" is the pin number!

-You've been together for years but he won't propose to you and he gives you excuses as to why. I'll tell you why: because he doesn't intend to marry you, he only intends to use you.

-Are you supporting his drug habit? Does he steal from your purse? Even if he cries and says sorry later... it's wrong.

Intuition: A Girl's Best Friend

There are three ways to know for sure if you need to take out your trash. The number one, easiest way to know for sure your man is a user or a loser is your intuition. Your intuition is screaming at you, "something isn't right here!!!" But, you ignore it. Your intuition is a gift from God. It will rarely steer you in the wrong direction. Nine out of ten times, your intuition will be right. Don't ignore it.

Second way to know for sure it's time to take out the trash is you're the one who puts in all the effort. Your relationship is not 50/50; it is more like 80/20. You're the one who's always calling him, picking up the tab, paying the bills, or taking all the shit.

The third for sure sign he needs to be kicked to the curb is when he refuses to show his affection for you. If he isn't at all affectionate in front of friends and family or if he won't even bring you around his friends and family; this is your cue that something is wrong. If he lies to people about your relationship, or says not to tell people about your relationship; whatever his excuse is for "hiding" you, don't fall for it. It's wrong and you don't deserve that.

You may be doubting what I'm telling you and wondering, "Well, then why is he around if he doesn't care about me?" "Why would he keep me around? He must like me a little?" Hear me loud and clear! He's only stringing you along, so you're there when he needs you. For whatever it might be. Even if it's just an emotional thing, he's still using you.

I'm sorry to say it, but if your man is doing any of the things listed in this chapter, don't fool yourself. That kind of man isn't interested in you as a person. He's only interested in getting what he wants, when he wants it. You getting hurt in the process is just a side effect. Your feelings are no concern of his. He pretends they are, but that's an act. He pretends to care or even love you but you know his actions speak the truth.

Chapter 6

THE POWER OF SELECTIVE ATTTRACTION

Forget about looks and a nice body. Being attracted to the superficial will ALWAYS leave you with a broken heart. You have to forget about the way a guy looks, what kind of car he drives, and how nice his body is. You have to forget about everything that's physically attractive about a man and become attracted to the way a man treats you. This whole chapter can be easily summarized in this one sentence:

You must be attracted to the way a man treats you, before you are attracted to ANYTHING else about him.

Please don't get this confused! I'm not saying a guy has to be ugly. I'm not advising you to avoid dating good-looking people. That's not at all what I'm saying. There are plenty of fine men in this world that will treat you like a princess.

I know this because I see them every where. I know this because I have one. I have a good man that treats me very well and he's very handsome. Before I met him, I'd made up my mind to only be attracted to men that treated me well. Therefore, I wouldn't even consider dating a man, no matter how fine he was; if he didn't treat me well, first and foremost.

Being treated well means different things to different women. I know some of you have been in such terrible relationships that having a man that doesn't cheat and lie is considered being treated well. Then there are other women whose definition of being treated well means being showered with gifts and getting their ass licked. We're all different and being treated well will have a different meaning to each of us.

I suggest you write a paragraph underneath your requirements list. Start the paragraph off with: "Being treated well means..." and finish that sentence with your own definition. Write down at least five sentences that start with, "Being treated well means..." Once you have it written down, you can see exactly what you require from a man before you'll even consider becoming attracted to him.

Tom, Dick, and Harry

I want to give you a concrete example. Let's say you have three men in your life: Tom, Dick, and Harry. There's Dick...who is fine as fuck, has a sexy ass body and drives a really nice car. Dick won't ask you out on formal dates. He barely opens doors for you. He rarely calls you. You're the one that's always calling him. To top it all off, Dick won't label you as his girlfriend.

Nevertheless, you want to be with Dick because Dick is sexy. Dick gets your heart beating. He gives you those exhilarating butterflies in your stomach. A lot of other girls want Dick too, so he's a fun challenge for you. You really want to pursue things with him.

Then there's Harry, who's a super sweetheart but he's not very good looking at all. You could never see yourself with him, but he's head over heels in love with you. Harry has been in love with you since the 7th grade, and would probably take a bullet for you. The only problem is you just don't have any feelings for him.

Then there's Tom, who's cute, but he isn't the kind of guy you would usually date. He has a nice job and he's in college, but he doesn't have a decent car or anything else worth mentioning. He's not very popular, either.

HOWEVER, Tom calls when he says he will. Tom helped you fix your car when it broke down. Tom takes you on nice dates and always holds the door open for you. Tom *wants* to spend his time with you. You could possibly see yourself with Tom, but you aren't as attracted to Tom as you are to fine ass Dick.

Which one are you going to choose? Which will you allow the honor of your presence? If you're a smart woman, you're attracted to the way a man treats you. Therefore, Dick is out of the picture immediately. It doesn't matter that he gives you butterflies in your stomach and gets your blood pumping, because you're a strong woman that controls her emotions!

Then there's sweet Harry; but there are absolutely no feelings for him. Well, you can't *force* yourself to like someone, no matter how well they treat you. So, good bye

Harry...

Being the wise woman you are, you decide you're going to give Tom your time and attention, even though he's not your typical kind of guy. You choose to be attracted to Tom and not Dick, because you're attracted to the way a man treats you before you're attracted to anything else.

Now that you've been on a few dates with Tom, you come to realize he's amazing. He does everything you ever wanted a man to do. He's romantic and courteous. He calls and texts you every day. He's ambitious and educated. You start looking back and suddenly Dick isn't so fine. Tom is the man. Tom is sexy, because Tom is a good man. Nothing should be more attractive to you than a GOOD man.

I threw poor Harry in there to show you that just because someone is a good man, doesn't mean you HAVE to be attracted to him. If you have a Harry in your life but you just don't like the man, there's nothing you should do about it. Don't force yourself to be with someone simply because he's good to you or he's in love with you.

What you should do is use balance. If you have a Tom in your life but you choose a Dick over him, then you'll get hurt and you deserve it. Do you know why you deserve to be hurt? Because you picked superficial bullshit over a GOOD man. You picked looks and status over a man that treated you right. **If you don't learn to be attracted to the way a man treats you, over all other things, then you are likely to get hurt over and over again.**

Don't Lower Your Standards

This is not to be confused with lowering your standards. You need to have standards as protection. The standards you came up with on your list are there to protect you from getting involved with bad men. We all need standards because it's important to weed out any potential assholes, users, abusers, and losers.

The real trick becomes picking and choosing a man who meets a majority of the standards which are important to you AND treats you the way you want to be treated. You may have to wait awhile for him to come around, but he will come. However, you'll never meet him if you're busy staying committed to a loser or you keep falling for sexy douche bags.

The bottom line is that a man's looks, body, car, money, and popularity need to be secondary to how he treats you. You need to say to yourself and to the men in your life, "The #1 thing that turns me on in a man is the way he treats me."

Once you believe it, you can vocalize it to any potential man in your life. If you believe it yourself, he'll believe you. If he believes you, he'll know he has to be a good man if he wants to be with you. The following are examples of things a good man will do:

How to Spot a Good Man

-He calls when he said he would.

-He doesn't stand you up to go with his friends.

-He isn't caught telling little lies.

-He wants to spend his time with you.

-He picks up the phone when you call.

-You can depend on him.

-He helps you with your problems.

-He doesn't disappear.

-He's waiting to have sex. He isn't pressuring you into sex.

-He's good to his Mom and/or kids.

-He's good to your Mom. (Respectful, courteous and helpful.)

-Yes, these kinds of men do exist! They aren't extinct. They are out there. I promise.

Mama's Boys

Another thing you should always pay close attention to is the way a man treats the important women in his life. A Mama's boy can be a bad thing, but in some cases it can be a good thing. It all depends on what kind of Mama's boy he is. Is he loving and helpful to his mother or is he spoiled and disrespectful to her?

Secretly watch how a man treats the woman who raised him. This shows you exactly how he treats a woman that he loves. If a man is overly dependent or rude to his mother, this a bad sign and you should run far away from him as fast as you can.

However, if he's very helpful, dependable, and loving to her then that's good news for you. If he helps her, appreciates her, and respect her... this says a lot about his character as a man.

It all boils down to one question. Do you want to pamper someone or do you want to be the one pampered? A man that treats his mother, sisters, daughters, and grandmother with love and respect will do the same for his wife.

How to Never Be Sad Over a Man Ever Again

If you decide that from now on you'll be attracted

to the way a man treats you, above all other superficial bullshit, you'll never be sad over a man again.

You'll always be happy.

You won't get used for sex. You will be asked out on dates. You won't cry. You won't be lied to, cheated on, ignored, or abused. You won't feel lonely. You'll be happy and respected by the men you allow into your life. All of these wonderful things will happen in your relationships, simply because you **choose** to only be attracted to men who treat you well.

Chapter 7

THE POWER OF ACTION

Have you ever heard the saying, "Don't talk about it, be about it"? That's one of my favorite sayings because it has so much meaning behind it. When it comes to love, that quote is right on the money. A person can say, "I love you" a million times and it means nothing. It's so easy to say. However, for a person to "love you" and put action behind their words, that's hard. That takes effort. That's because love is an action.

Men Lie About Love

If you have a man telling you he loves you, but his actions are saying something different, then it's time to realize that he's lying to you. If you feel sad on a regular basis, he doesn't love you. To be blunt, he doesn't even care! If you're being lied to, cheated on, or abused in any way; whether physically, emotionally, or verbally...that man does NOT love you.

Love is an action and when a person really loves you, they'll show it. Just like when you love a person, you don't hurt them. When you love a man, you don't lie to him or cheat on him. You might do those things to a man you don't really care about, but not a man you love.

If you wouldn't treat someone you love that way; why do you believe a man, who treats you badly, actually loves you? Is the man in your life showing you he loves you, or is he just saying it?

You believe him because he's saying it, but men

have a different mindset than us. They can say, "I love you" and not mean it at all! They do it all the time and don't feel one bit guilty about it. Women, on the other hand, would feel terribly guilty to do something like that. That's why it's so hard for us to believe a man is lying when he says it. If we even tried to lie to a guy about loving him, we would feel so bad about it. They don't.

Men lie about loving us. They lie about caring about us. They lie about it all the time, and they do it without remorse. They do it for one reason: they want to have sex. They do it all for the nookie. They're on a mission. A mission to stick their dick inside of you.

How to Know When a Man Loves You

If men lie about loving us, how can we ever tell when a man sincerely loves us? It's very easy to tell when a man really loves you. When a man cares about you, *you will see it in his actions*. He may not even have to say "I love you" or "I care about you." You know he does by the way he acts.

He's reliable. He's honest. He calls when he says he will, and he picks up the phone when you call. If it goes to voice mail, he calls you right back as soon as he can. He *wants* to spend time with you. He brings surprises for you or your kids. He takes you out.

He introduces you to his family and friends. He shows you off. He has no problem leaving his friends behind to come spend time with you. He realizes how special you are. He sees what you have to offer. He values you and he values his time with you.

If he isn't doing things like this, he doesn't care about you. He's just enjoying having you there when he needs you for sex or whatever else you may be providing. Don't try to convince yourself otherwise. I understand sometimes it's confusing to tell if his actions are sincere. A lot of the time men will put on a show in the beginning of the relationship in an effort to convince you they are a good guy. They will literally trick you into having sex with them. Then once you do, all the nice gestures stop.

There's an easy way around this. Don't have sex with him! Remember, if you like a guy, you should *hold out*. Make him wait at least two months. If, at the end of two months, he's still displaying that he cares, I would say he's sincere.

Most men will give up after the first few weeks or the first few dates, unless you're giving in by giving him oral sex or hand jobs. STOP IT! No sex in the first 60 days! Listen, if you want to know if this person is sincere, you have to make him prove himself. He can't prove himself if you're giving him blow jobs.

Could You Be That One Special Girl?

If 60 days have passed and you're still having a hard time trying to figure out if his actions are sincere, then remember to see if he'll come to your rescue like Prince Charming. If a man really likes you, even if he only cares for you and doesn't love you yet, he'll want to come to your rescue. This is what men do naturally. We are the nurturers and they are the protectors. Men are our knights in shining armor, **but they'll only do it for one special girl.**

They like to help the ones they love because it makes them feel like an alpha male — needed and appreciated. If he does come to your rescue, it's time to thank him for all of his effort. **Be appreciative and give him some praise for helping you.**

Men like to be appreciated, just like women. You don't need to over exaggerate. Just being thankful and appreciative is enough. You can even reward him, wink wink, for being such a good man. That's your way of letting your actions speak to him.

Chapter 8

THE POWER OF KEEPING YOURSELF BUSY

It's important if you want to be a strong woman who is respected by the men in her life, that you keep yourself busy. By busy, I mean in school or working on your career. I'm not referring to hanging out on the corner with your friends all day. I'm not referring to going to a club every other night.

Nothing turns a man on more than a woman with a *life of her own*. A woman who has goals and dreams. A woman with a nice career. Don't you like a man with these attributes? Men like it even more, because men are show offs.

The Type of Women Men Love

When a woman has her own things going on, it's a big turn on to a man. Why? It makes a man take interest. He sees a woman who doesn't need or want a man. He sees a smart, hard worker, who has her own life. A woman that's busy and has to be choosy about who she spends her time with.

Being busy and having your own life is important for several reasons. The most important reason: **Men want what they can't have.** You have to be so preoccupied with your own life that men can't get to your time, let alone your heart without some effort. Plain and simple.

Why They Want Her

An independent woman doesn't rely on a man to fill in her life for her. She's not the clingy or overbearing type. She's not searching in desperation for love. She's not on a hunt to find "the one." She's not looking to get married or in a hurry to have kids.

Men run far away from those kinds of women. **They want the opposite of that**. They want a woman who's so busy with her own life, she doesn't even want a man. Therefore, since the man can't have her, it makes him want her. Getting her to notice him and fall in love with him becomes his goal. (Notice that we do this too. When a man we like doesn't show the same interest in a commitment, it becomes our ultimate goal to get him to "settle down".)

You want to be the one that is being chased for a commitment, not the other way around. This is actually the natural order of love. The men are supposed to be the ones pursuing us and convincing us that they are worthy. Somewhere along the way shit got all twisted around. We have become the ones pushing for commitment and marriage. We need to flip it back around to the natural order to correct this dysfunction.

Cats don't chase dogs.

Dogs chase cats.

Remember that.

You want to be so busy and proactive in your own life that you don't need a man, nor want a man, because you don't have time for a man. Your time is valuable and therefore, men will know not to waste it. You won't even allow them to waste it.

When a man sees a woman with no time to waste, he'll cut to the chase. He won't beat around the bush, trying to run game to get you into bed. He'll do things the proper way and ask you out on a date.

He'll try to impress you, so you'll want to spend *your* time with *him*. Instead of it being the other way around, where you're the one trying to get him to spend *his* time with *you*.

He'll want your time, because it's not easy to get. You'll become the type of woman that men don't string along. To be that type of woman, you need to have *your own life*. If you've been debating about whether or not to go back to school, just do it. If you've wanted to set some goals, but haven't done it yet, just do it. It's time to become "that type of woman." A woman that has HER OWN IMPORTANT LIFE and therefore has no time or desire for a man, let alone a man playing games.

It's all about how you perceive yourself. If you want to be a strong woman, you need to demonstrate you are indeed a strong woman. Strong women have their own things going on. Again, that doesn't mean hanging out and going to clubs every night. You need to have some valuable life goals that you're working on (if you don't already). By having these goals, you're making a strong statement to the men in your life. You're saying:

"No one is more important than me."

"I don't have time for games."

"When you're with me, you better make it worth my time, or I won't waste my time with you the next time I'm free."

"I have a lot to offer."

"I require respect because I respect myself enough to make a better life for myself."

"I can take care of myself and I don't NEED a man."

"If I choose to be with you, it is because I wanted to be with you, not because I needed to be with you."

Very Important Questions

This book is about learning what men want and using it to get the love you desire. I'm going to go off topic for one moment to speak about goals. Some of you have your goals figured out or have even accomplished them already, and if you have, that's great! I want you to take this moment to pat yourself on the back. You're one step ahead of the game. You're also serving as motivation to women all around you. Congratulations on accomplishing any goal, because not everyone does. You should feel very proud of yourself.

However, some of you are just strolling along, day after day, not working toward anything. Set some goals and work hard toward these goals. Anything worth having in life is going to take some hard work.

You should take a moment to think about what you want your life and your future to be like. Ask yourself some very important questions and answer them in your journal:

Where do you see yourself in one year?

Where do you see yourself in five years?

Where do you see yourself in ten years?

What is your dream career?

How much money do you want to earn per year?

How do you envision your future?

What steps will it take to get there?

Make sure your goals are practical and achievable, but **don't be afraid to set big goals**. Now write out 1-year goals, 5-year goals, and 10-year goals. Write out what kind of work it will require to get there. Now, do the work and accomplish the goals! It could be as simple as losing weight and as complex as becoming a doctor. Whatever it is, you can do it!

Dream big, believe that you can do it, and most importantly, work hard. If you do those three things. I promise you can accomplish anything. My best friend dreamed of being an airline pilot, but thought it would be an impossible mission. She decided not to give into her doubts. She dreamed big, set the goal, did the hard work and became a pilot. Here we are eight years later and she now flies huge passenger jets around the world for great money.

You can do anything you want in this life. Why not make it something special? I've set several goals in my life, and I've accomplished a majority of them. Sometimes people laughed at my goals, but I kept working and I eventually accomplished them.

At 21, I became an on-air radio personality at Power 96 in Miami. At 26, I invested in real estate and opened my own business. I went to college. I learned to speak Spanish. I wrote a book. I am not telling you this to brag. I am telling you this because I want you to know for a fact that you can do whatever you set your mind to. As long as you set the goal, believe you can achieve it and then do the work to get there...anything is possible.

What's amazing is the goals always seems so far away, but they're usually accomplished in less time than you originally estimated. I gave myself a time line of five years to get my own radio show. It happened in 18 months. Before my friend started working on her goal to be a pilot, we both assumed she would be in her 40's before she'd make it to the airlines. She was 27.

You feel like goals will take years and years, and in reality it happens a lot faster than you think! It's the "work" part that gets in a lot of people's way. They dream big, but don't ever do the physical work behind the goal. Life doesn't work that way. Life rewards action. Remember my favorite saying, "Don't talk about it, be about it"?

For example, I used to dream about writing this book. One day I decided I was tired of talking about it and I was just going to do it. Do you think writing this book came easily? I've been **working** on this book for three years. Three years of grueling, disciplined, hard work.

It's easy to TALK about big goals. It's not easy to do the WORK it takes to reach the big goals but the WORK is the only way the goal can be achieved. It's easier to fail than it is to succeed. Success takes work, hard work. How hard are you willing to WORK to be the woman you desire to be?

I can tell you that no matter who you dream of becoming, it is attainable. The same goes for being a strong, independent woman. If you really want to be a bad ass, independent woman that doesn't take shit from men; you need to do the work behind it.

So, let's say you've always wanted to finish high school, go to college, and become a pediatric nurse so that you could work in the NICU. It seems like such a far away goal, so you convince yourself it will never happen...and so, it never does.

Now let's say you choose a different attitude. You decide you're going to stop talking about it and just do it. So, now you're enrolled in GED classes and you're focused on your goal. You don't have time to waste on losers because you have more important things going on. So, eventually you get your GED and now you're in college.

You're working towards your goal while managing to avoid getting involved with any jerks (because you don't have time for that crap). You only have time open for good men who earn your time. When you do date, the guy will be honored to be dating "an intelligent and independent woman who's in college, becoming a nurse." He'll brag to his family and friends about you.

Therefore, it's a win-win situation. You're becoming a better person, and doing some things you always dreamed of doing. At the same time, you're sending a clear message to any potential mates that you're valuable, and you won't be an easy catch. Any man who wants you better come correctly. He will formally ask you out if he wants your time. He'll be a perfect gentleman, because a woman like you will take nothing less.

Dick = Distraction

An important thing to remember is not to get involved with a goal and meet a good man and lose focus. Sometimes love makes us forget about our own personal goals. You get involved with a man and get carried away. You miss a day of school here and there and before you know it, you've stopped going to school.

You want to spend all of your time with this great person. STOP IT! You're losing yourself and you'll eventually turn this guy off by smothering him and losing yourself in him. Don't let the dick be a distraction from your personal goals. Be careful and don't make that mistake. It happens to women all the time, so be prepared to control yourself and stay focused when this happens!

Stay focused on your own life. Don't use a man as a way to fill in your life for you. **This makes you the clingy, overbearing girl and it pushes men away.** If you have no goals or ambition and find it hard to keep yourself busy, the next chapter will give you one sure way to fill your time repeatedly. You can use the next chapter as a way to fill your time, so you keep yourself busy and appear to be unattainable.

Chapter 9

THE POWER OF THE SUPER DATER

Want to have men lining up to date you? Would you enjoy an endless stream of men telling you how beautiful you are and that they'd love to spend some time with you? By the time you're done with this chapter, all of that will be easily within reach. By the time you're through with this book you'll become a super dater, with men lined up to date you. How? Two words. **Online Dating.**

How to Have Men Lining Up To Date You

It's vital that I include a chapter about online dating because it's the new way of doing things. More importantly, when done right, online dating will provide you with a mass of men waiting in line to date you. When online dating first began back in the late 90's, it was kind of a desperate way of dating, much like taking out a single's ad in the paper. Now, it's the normal way of meeting people in this age of technology. This is great news for you!

Don't feel bad about online dating *at all*. Don't feel like a loser because you choose to date online. That cliche is dead. This is the way it's done now. If you haven't tried it in the past, it's time to try it out. This chapter will guide and direct you through it all. If you have tried it and been unsuccessful, this chapter will give you the proper guidance needed to be an online dating professional.

Online dating is great for women. We have an advantage. It all comes back to the power of the pussy. Simply because we're women, online dating is usually free for us. More importantly, we have the upper hand in the online dating world, just as we do in the real world. But, just like the real world, you can only have the upper hand if you know what you're doing. I'm going to guide and direct you in a way that will teach you step by step how to control your online dating experiences.

To start off, you want to join an online dating site that's free for women. Just type in a search engine, "Online Dating Free for Women." A ton of dating sites that are free for women will pop up. First join one, then over time, join others.

The more you join, the more men you'll have lining up to date you. So, what kind of dater do you want to be? Do you want to be a super dater, that has men lined up waiting? Or, do you just want one casual date a month? Join as many sites as it takes to get you where you want to be.

So, you want to start off with the free sites. Once you're comfortable engaging with men online, then move to the paid sites. The reason you want to eventually land on the paid sites is because you get what you pay for. On the paid sites, you have a higher quality group of men compared to the free sites. I'm not saying there aren't good men on the free ones, but there's definitely a better pool of guys to pick from on the paid sites. Below is a list of dating sites to choose from.

Here are some free dating sites

(These Sites Have Quantity Over Quality):

Plenty Of Fish (pof.com)

OKCupid.com

Here are the higher quality, paid dating sites

(These Sites Have Quality Over Quantity):

Match.com

eHarmony.com

Sometimes paid sites have free weekends. Look out for the commercials on television, as they usually promote the free weekends before they do it. You can also go directly to the site and visit their FAQ or contact them to ask when the free trial weekend will happen.

Now, let's talk about your online dating ad. This is an advertisement. You are selling yourself. You should act accordingly. This doesn't mean you should be someone else or put on an act. You just need to be the best version of yourself. It's the same in the real world. I don't know why people get an online dating ad and then forget to hold back. You wouldn't divulge everything about yourself when first meeting someone in person, so why do that in your online ad?

For example, some women go off in their online dating ad about how they "just got divorced and have a bit more to love." Sorry, but that's just too much of the wrong information upfront. You're supposed to be SELLING yourself.

A good online dating ad should describe all of the great things about you. Leave out the negative. I had a client that had an online dating account that said all these great things. Then, at the very end it said something like, "a little chubby, but still cute." She didn't understand why she wasn't getting very many responses.

Would you want to date a guy whose ad said, "I'm a little chubby, but still cute"? NO...don't even pretend. Human beings are superficial. Even the nice human beings are judgmental and superficial. It's natural for us to judge people when first meeting or learning about a person. Once we make a connection and we like the person we tend to overlook the negative. So, wait until you've grabbed a man's attention before divulging all of your baggage.

NEVER EVER say "a bit more to love" or "a little chubby." Remember the chapter on self-esteem? Even when you're comfortable with a person, these types of comments must be kept to yourself. Break the habit of putting your self down.

I made my client change her ad. We made it say

nothing negative about herself. In fact, we even added some sexual undertones with a line that said, "Sexy lips and nice hips." Why would I be so graphic? Remember, we're advertising to men! Men thrive on sexual stimulation. The next day she had twelve messages in her inbox! All different kinds of men asking her for more info or straight up asking if she'd like to go out sometime.

By taking the focus off the negative and turning it around to a sexual positive, she was able to stimulate their minds and gain interest. Some of you will think that's wrong, but you need to understand the way men think. They lose interest easily. Sexual notations done in a subtle way catches their eye.

Now you're thinking, "Well, now they'll just be interested in sex." Oh well! They can be interested in sex all day and night, but it doesn't mean that's what they'll get. In fact, it's good to make them subconsciously think about sex. Then they'll try even harder to impress you!

You just can't be direct about it. You can't say, "single lady looking for a good time with sexy lips and nice hips." However, by leaving out the first part and just including a good quality description of yourself with light sexual undertones; you'll get their attention without leading them to believe you're an easy target for sex.

Now that she has twelve responses in her inbox, she can go through the list of responses and decide which man she'll go out with. Instead of it being the other way around, where she was waiting for the men to choose her. she has the control now. You'll need to gain and maintain the control when dating in the real world or online.

I know it seems hard at first, but the steps to maintaining the control are basic: Know that simply because you have a vagina, that makes you valuable. Don't ever forget this! Don't put yourself down, EVER. Change your perception: you are a prize to be won, and the best man wins the prize. Don't let men into your life who aren't willing to work to win you over.

Make them work for it and make them work HARD for it. If he doesn't want to work for it, let him walk and move onto the next man. If you get hung up on a guy you like and find it hard to let him go, control those emotions! Move on to the next player. Stay single for as long as you can. Date a lot of different men and date them all at one time! Don't settle down easily.

This works in the real world and it works in the online dating world. It takes practice but with time, it will become easier and second nature to you. When it does, you will be overwhelmed with excitement. Dating will become fun and you'll feel so empowered! It's really a great feeling. You'll never look at men the same way again.

Dating with Balance

Now we need to talk seriously for a minute. Some of you aren't going to like this part coming up because I'm going to be perfectly honest. I'm probably going to hurt someone's feelings. I don't care. Some of you need to hear this! Let's talk about standards. Some of you have your standards too high and some of you have your standards too low.

Those of you who have your standards too high, you know who you are. You go for the fine guys. You only date the good-looking, perfect body guys. Then you wonder why the men in your life are always assholes and why they're all dicks.

Why do they lie? Why do they cheat? Why, Why, Why? Maybe it's time to lower your overly-high standards in an effort to catch a good man. He may not be the perfect 10 you were looking for, but he's the one that will be good to you.

He's the one that won't hesitate to take you out to nice restaurants and open doors for you, which the "perfect 10" guy would NEVER think of doing. He just may be the faithful, honest, and caring man you hope for... but you'll never know because you're too busy being vain and dating good-looking jerks!

I'm sorry, but it's time for someone to say it. You don't have the right to be so picky. You aren't perfect. Why should you expect perfection? You're only sabotaging yourself. You're missing out on all of the millions of good men out there, just because they don't have a six-pack and a Brad Pitt face. Do you find yourself wondering where all the good men are? They're there. You just won't date them!

There are some honest, faithful, wonderful guys in this world. Women pass them up all the time, because "he's too short" or "he's too chubby." We'll always find something wrong with a man. Take notice and stop yourself when you're being too judgmental.

Then there are the women on the other end of the spectrum. Some of you have your standards so ass backwards, you go after the first guy that pays you a tiny bit of attention. It happens all the time, in all kinds of settings. It could be the first online dating message you get in your inbox, you reply to it immediately.

Or worse, the first new guy that comes around, you immediately start catching feelings for him. You start plotting with your friends how you're going to approach the new guy. It could be the new guy in town, or the new guy at school, or the new guy at work. You get all excited and become a fool, ready to rush in. Or, it could be the guy that talked to you at the party last weekend, so you think, "he must like me." Then you automatically start having a crush on this stranger.

This is all wrong! You don't need to be so desperate. This desperation is killing your chances from the start. Remember, you're a woman. You're a lady. Ladies don't chase after men. Men come to women. It is unnatural for a woman to search in desperation for a man.

Men want what they can't have. They only want you when you don't want them. By pursuing the man, you're automatically turning him off. You're actually doing the worst thing you could possibly do. This method will never work.

If you follow the methods laid out in this book, you'll be able to *draw the man to you*. In addition, if he isn't automatically drawn towards you, you'll need to forget about him and move on. Because this means he was never interested in you in the first place. You can now avoid all the heartache that comes along with pursuing a man that doesn't want you.

Doesn't it absolutely suck when you start liking a guy only to find out he has a girlfriend? Or even worse, he flat out tells someone he doesn't like you? Avoid the embarrassment and heartache by controlling yourself and conducting yourself as a lady. Ladies don't pursue men.

You need to find a nice balance. Don't search for perfection and be overly critical of men. Moreover, don't be the opposite of that, open to dating whoever looks your way. A nice balance will keep your head out of the clouds and keep you grounded.

Thank you for allowing me to get that out, it needed to be said. Now, back to online dating. When you start online dating, go into it with an open mind. I want you to look at dating a variety of guys. Date older guys, date younger guys, date fine guys, date ugly guys, date tall guys and then date short guys. Stop going after that certain type of guy you always go for, it's time to change it up. Open your mind to a new kind of dating experience by dating a wide variety of men.

YOU DON'T HAVE TO BE PHYSICALLY ATTRACTED TO SOMEONE TO GO ON A SIMPLE DATE WITH THEM.

It's not a big deal. You aren't stuck with the person forever... it's just a date. And hey, guess what? Men do this all the time! Many men are open to dating all kinds of women. They like variety and you should too. I think they do it for different reasons, like raising their chances of getting laid, but whatever. You're going to do it because you want to have a lot of dates.

Having a lot of dates is not only fun, it fills your time and makes you and your time more valuable. You're also going to do it because then you'll have a wide range of men playing the "who can win her love" game. The more, the merrier.

Remember they're just pots on a stove. You want to be dating two to four guys at any one time. There will be ones you like a lot. The others you don't like so much will serve as back-ups. It's really not a big deal. You aren't going to marry them or have sex with them; it's just a date. You don't even have to finish the date if you don't want to.

Don't Be Afraid To Get Up and Leave

One time I went out with a guy who wasn't my type because he was preppy and he was a little overweight. I honestly didn't care because I had decided to give all kinds of men a chance. Well, at dinner he said something very rude to me. He said, "I usually date girls smaller than you."

I was thinking to myself, "Can you believe the nerve of this guy to insult me? Look who's talking!" I thought about what I should say in response. I decided not to say anything. I smiled and then I politely excused myself from the table, as if I had to use the restroom. Then I snuck away to my car and I left him sitting there by himself. I couldn't believe I had the balls to do that to him. But I'm glad I did it and I don't regret it. It was very amusing and he deserved it.

Don't hesitate to do the same, because you're a beautiful woman and you don't need to take that kind of crap from anyone. He sent me an email the next day insulting me. I just deleted it and blocked his email address. Now, I could have chosen to let it hurt my feelings, but I controlled my emotions. Because I know that I'm a beautiful woman, even if I'm not a size 4. Besides, I had five new emails in my inbox from men wanting to meet me and my glorious figure!

If you're on a date with a guy who annoys you or is rude to you, don't hesitate to excuse yourself like I did. (You'll get a good laugh and it'll be a funny story to tell your friends.) Never feel obligated to a guy because he's paying for dinner. You're not there for his entertainment. He's there to impress you, and if he doesn't want to play that game, then no more of your time shall be wasted on him.

You're going to run into assholes like that, it's inevitable. You've probably already dated jerks like that. Just keep on moving and don't let it bother you. The old saying holds true, "plenty of fish in the sea." One fish might think you're fat, and the next fish might think you're a curvaceous beauty. Don't waste your time on men who see you as anything less than the goddess you are.

When dating a variety of men you're going to end up dating a few ugly ducklings, a few jerks that make you sick, or a few men that bore you to death. You might date a guy that talks too much, or a guy that is beyond annoying. You might find a man that's just like you and fall madly in love. Who knows what you'll find out there. But, you'll never know if you don't get out there and start dating different kinds of men!

Online Dating Is Important To You For Several Reasons:

You're in control because the men are seeking you out.

You have tons of options.

You can have several dates lined up immediately.

Once you have many dates lined up, you don't have a lot of time to waste. So, you're keeping yourself busy and "unavailable," which is just what men love.

Men don't need to know you're busy because you're dating a lot. Just say you're busy, they don't need an explanation. Remember, men hate hearing about other men! You shouldn't lie and pretend he's the only man you're seeing, but you don't need to provide details.

There's a way you can avoid getting into details, without lying about your dating life. If the topic comes up, brush it off by simply saying you're a single woman who's "enjoying her freedom". That way you're being honest about your dating life, without saying, "Hey, I'm dating three different guys this week and you're just another guy in the long line of men waiting to win me over." You want to let this be known, without saying it.

You'll let him know this by the vibe you let off, not with words. It's perfectly fine to let it be known you're single, because then the guy thinks he has a chance and he'll try hard to get you. However, if he finds out he's just another chump in the line of men you're dating, he'll probably lose interest.

Find a well-balanced statement that works well for

you. However, you must avoid saying things like, "I'm single and just looking to have fun," or you'll automatically be labeled as a booty call. Something about the word "fun" translates into "sex" in man language. Don't use that line in your online dating ad or your inbox will get FLOODED with pervs trying to screw you.

When you do start getting responses in your inbox, it's important to remember a few things. Never go out with a guy for "coffee" or "a walk in the park" unless you want to. This means he's either broke or just plain cheap. To weed through the cheapskates, always use the "I'm a lady" excuse. You can say, "I prefer to go on formal dates."

He'll either step his game up and take you out somewhere nice or he'll go away. If he goes away, good! You just avoided dating a cheapskate. You avoided dating a man that thought if he bought you some coffee, he could screw you with minimal effort. REMEMBER: If he isn't interested in putting in any effort, he's just a player out there looking to wham-bam, thank you ma'am. Let him go...

Now, you might find a broke guy that you REALLY like. He might be honest and upfront, "Hey, I'm in college and I don't have much money, but could I take you out, maybe to the park for a picnic?" If you really like him and he comes off as an honest guy and you don't mind, then give him a chance. It's not about how much they spend on you, it's about their intentions.

Keep an eye out for the cheap assholes, because

there are a lot of them out there trying to get by on women. They get sick of always paying for dinner and not getting laid so they try the cheap version of dating. You just have to let it be known you're not that kind of girl. If he doesn't want to step up and pay, ignore him and let it go. He might change his mind and come back with a counter offer.

Keep the Pussy Safe!

Online dating and safety go hand in hand. Some of the safety tips listed below should be common sense, but sometimes we forget. Some of us are too trusting of people. Some of us are going to be too scared to ever consider online dating. It's my opinion that online dating is completely safe, if you use caution and common sense.

Just because you meet someone online doesn't mean they're going to be a crazy stalker. Someone you meet at the grocery store can be just as dangerous as an online dater. No matter where or how you meet men, in order to protect yourself from potential predators, you should follow these rules when you begin dating a man.

-Never display or give away your full name or address.

-Make calls from your cell phone, that way if you do give a guy your number, you can always change the number easily. It's okay to give out your cell number, if your real name is not on the caller ID and you don't mind changing the number if you have to. Nowadays, some cell phone companies let you put just your first name or a nickname as the display on the caller ID. Inquire with your cell phone company about this, and tell them it's for privacy issues.

-Alternatively, you can ask for his number and call from an unknown number (dial *67 before dialing his number and it will block your number). Do this until you feel comfortable with him. Once you trust the man, you can give him your number. It's okay to be honest, tell him you're sorry you have to call from an unknown number, but you have to consider your personal safety when dating online. He should understand and respect that.

-Always meet in very public places. Restaurants inside of malls are always a good idea. Plan to meet inside of the public place and not in the parking lot. Don't ever let him walk you to the car alone at night, when no one is around. If you don't have a car, find a public place in walking distance and meet there. NEVER allow a man to pick you up at your home, friends/family home, school, place of business or anywhere he can trace you back to if things don't work out.

-Always tell someone WHO you are going out with, WHERE you're going, and WHEN you'll be home. Give this person whatever information you have about the guy. Tell them you'll call them once you're home safe, and don't forget to call them or they might worry themselves sick all night!

-Use a designated email address for dating. You can get free email addresses at hotmail.com and gmail.com. You must do this, especially if you have a business email or an email address that links to personal information. For example, if a man puts your email address into a Google search, and your email is somehow linked to your personal info via a website or business site; he can find out whatever info is out there about you. (You can also reverse this and do it yourself to find out info about the guys you date!)

An Important Note About
Email Addresses And User Names

Please don't make your new email address something too sexual, such as:

hotgirl69@gmail.com

SexxxyThangIzAFreak@hotmail.com

You're a lady! Remember? Your email should be classy, like you! Try an email related to your "offerings." If you're in college, CollegeGirl@hotmail.com would be okay because it's flirty, without being trashy.

I know I told you to use some sexual undertones. The keyword being *undertones*. You have to be sexual in a non-obvious way. Men think of sex when they see college girl. Women would never see that as sexual, but men do! Therefore, it isn't very hard to get the sexual undertone in there without saying it directly.

Another thing to avoid is being too cutesy or desperate.

Referring to email addresses such as:

Looking4Love@gmail.com or

LongWalksOnTheBeach@aol.com

I don't know why, but things like that scare men away. I think they automatically see someone looking to get married and so they stray away from it. Stick to using your "offerings" as a base for the email address and/or user name.

Here are some good examples of emails that will work:

If you are a nurse: NurseLady24@hotmail.com

Generic: AshleyIsSingle@hotmail.com

If you're an office worker: BusinessWoman09@gmail.com

Or, be creative: BeautifulStranger@gmail.com or
ClassyGirl25@gmail.com

None of those email address ideas that I listed have anything sexual to them (to a woman), but to a man he sees this:

For CollegeGirl: He sees a young co-ed in a t-shirt and panties, bouncing around her dorm room.

For NurseLady: He sees a sexy nurse, with the stethoscope and skimpy white uniform.

For AshleyIsSingle: He sees a hot young girl named Ashley.

For BusinessWoman: He sees a sexy woman in a business suit and high heels.

It's just the way their minds work. They're automatically associating things with sex *all day long*. The point is you don't have to put much effort into getting the undertones in there. But, you shouldn't ever put things like 69 or freaky girl. That will automatically say, "I'm looking for sex. Who wants to do me?"

I hope these safety precautions don't scare you away from online dating. There's a world of dating potential just waiting for you out there! With online dating, you can have five dates lined up in a matter of days. It's like an endless supply of men. So, please don't be frightened by the online world. Remember, you can meet psychos at the grocery store as easily as you can online.

The men online are not weird or psychopaths because they are online. The majority of them are regular guys. Some are online because it's simply easier for them to date that way. Rejection isn't as fierce via email as it is in person.

Go easy on men that date online. They do it because it's an easier, more comfortable way for them to talk to women. Not because they're losers with bad intentions. Although there is a always some online, and in the real world, that are losers with bad intentions! Take the safety precautions seriously, don't be naïve, and ALWAYS USE COMMON SENSE.

Chapter 10

THE POWER OF ACTING LIKE A MAN

When all else fails, just act like a man. If it's hard for you to do many of the things in this book, always stick to the "Act Like A Man" approach. Ask yourself, would a man do this? How would a guy handle this? Do all of the things in this book *and* act like a man. Acting like a man means to handle dating and love the way a man would. Here's a detailed list of what men do, that we don't, but we should do...

What Men Do That We Don't Do

Men don't get emotionally involved. They keep their emotions at a distance and keep them hidden away. Most of the time they don't even have any feelings or emotions towards a girl. Very rarely will they allow emotions to come into play. Men keep that stuff locked away until they know for sure they love the girl. You need to do the same thing. Keep your emotions and feelings at a distance and don't allow them in until you know for sure the guy is worth it.

Men don't dwell on the small stuff. They don't sit around and over-analyze all the details. When you find yourself contemplating every little detail, stop it! Do what men do...relax. Simply put, don't give a shit about a guy. Guys don't give a shit about the girls they date. Be like a guy.

Men don't try to fix a woman. We're always trying to "fix" our guy. We get with a guy and think we can rescue him. We may not even realize we're doing this, but we do it all the time. We think, "I'll help him get back in school" or "I'll help him find a good job." Or even worse, we end up picking up all the slack for him. He doesn't have a place to live, so you let him live with you for free. He doesn't have a job, so you give him some cash here and there. Guys don't do this! Unless it's an old guy and a young pretty girl.

Men don't try to rationalize being treated badly. If a woman is treating a man badly or cheating on him, he'll leave her alone. We, on the other hand, could be dating a complete asshole and we'll put up with a ton of crap before we finally get the courage or strength to leave. Guys don't do this. They don't take crap. If a woman starts treating them badly, they'll leave her alone and move on to the next woman without a second thought about it. If a woman cheats on them, they move on. It hurts them just like it hurts us, but they rarely stick around for it to happen again.

Men separate the "wife" from the "booty call." We try to turn booty calls into love. Men have women they love and women they just use for sex. We try to get emotionally involved with whoever pays attention to us. We need to be more like men, and save the love and emotions for someone worthy of the title "husband."

Men think with their dicks, not their hearts.
Occasionally they will think using their head over their dicks, but *never* their hearts! Therefore, you should start to think like a man, by NOT thinking with your heart. When faced with a dilemma, stop thinking with your heart and use your head.

Men gather a bunch of "cool stuff" to make them more appealing to the opposite sex. They get nice cars and hook them up with nice rims, so that girls will sweat them. They buy expensive clothes and shoes. They stay focused on making money. They do all of this in order to look good to the opposite sex and attract women to them like magnets. It works very well for them.

So, you should be like a man. Gather a bunch of "cool stuff," so that men will sweat you. If you already have it, then be aware of it's worth to the opposite sex. Stop worrying about finding a guy with a car and go get yourself a nice ass car! The men will flock to you, the way we flock to men with these things. Men aren't the only ones who can buy cars and hook them up. You can do this too, and you should! Not just to attract men, but to boost your own self worth and feel great about yourself.

Don't Get This Chapter Confused

Please don't get this chapter confused. I said, "Act like a man," I did NOT say, "be one of the guys." **DO NOT** try to fit in with the guys. I don't want you to pretend you like sports or fishing. Don't start drinking beer and belching while watching football. Don't join in the sex conversation and talk about your sexual encounters as if you were a guy.

I'm only asking that you apply some of the unique qualities that men possess when dating. Men hate it when girls try to act like one of the guys, unless she's being herself and she's naturally that way. However, a man can tell when a girl is just trying to impress him or when she's just trying to be cute. When she sits and watches the game and pretends she's into it, when he knows and she knows she'd rather be watching *The Notebook*.

You should never pretend to be someone you're not for a guy. It turns him off, makes you look stupid, and it just won't work. Say you like a guy, and he's really into baseball. You don't really give a shit about baseball, but you really like this guy. You ask if you can come watch the game with him. You even buy a team shirt. You get all cute and dressed up.

You show up to the game looking great. But all he sees is a dumb ass trying to fit in and look cool. Unless your boobs are popping out of the team shirt, he couldn't care less. You're always better off being yourself. Now, if you naturally love baseball, that's fine, enjoy the game and be yourself. That he will appreciate. But no fakers, please.

There are many women in this world that try to change who they are to transform into the woman their man wants. This is the absolute wrong thing to do. You're going to make yourself uncomfortable for the entire relationship. Eventually you'll get sick of trying to be someone you're not. It will never work because in the end, someone is going to get sick of it. Either he'll begin to see through you, and be turned off, or you're going to get so sick of playing a role, you'll give up.

Flipping the Music Around

Music is a great tool to help you through any situation. I want to discuss how music can help you with the Power of Acting Like Man. A lot of people perceive rap music as degrading to women. In reality, it's empowering to women. I know that may seem hard to believe to those who don't appreciate the genre, but hear me out on this one.

People who don't listen to hip hop, don't understand that words such as bitch, trick, and ho are unisex words in hip hop. To women that listen to rap music, degrading words like bitch and ho are flipped around and applied to men. When I'm singing along to a rap song that says something like, "fuck all these hoes, I have no love for you bitches," I'm thinking of men, not women! It may sound crazy, but it's very empowering!

Now, think about it. A man may not technically be a person exchanging money for sex, but he's a ho nonetheless. *If he's not a good man or a man you love, then give him the same respect men give "hoes." Until you LOVE a man, he's just another HO to you.* When you listen to these songs, keep that in your head. Switch the meaning of the degrading words to represent the male species and watch how your attitude changes towards men!

For example, one of the songs I have listed is JT Money's "Ho Problems." This song is about a man telling other males to stop wasting their time getting upset over cheating, unfaithful women and let them go. The lyrics say:

"Ho problems, ain't no problems.
Go on and hate the game, but that ain't gonna solve it.
You need to learn when to let these mother fuckers go...

When are you gonna learn to let a ho be a ho?"

Now turn those lyrics around. Men are just hoes, remember! If a man is cheating on you and you're having a hard time leaving him, this is the perfect song to help you get over it! You need to learn to let that mother fucker go! When you gonna learn to let a ho be a ho? He's just a cheating, unfaithful ho, so let him go! Ho problems ain't no problems! Especially not for you. Not anymore.

I HIGHLY suggest every woman listen to this song **with the perspective flipped** because after listening to it enough times, it will completely change the way you think about men. That song is virtually impossible to find, it's somewhat of an underground song. I can't believe I found it on Amazon. So, if you want it, there's a link to it on the next page.

On the list of songs below, I have included the chapter and/or the topic it will help you with in parenthesis. I suggest you make a play list or a CD of just these songs (and any other songs that make you feel empowered). Music is therapy. Put these songs on when you're having a bad day, you need a boost in confidence, or you just need some extra support.

Some of the songs below are rap, please don't be annoyed because I'm asking you to listen to rap if it's not your thing. I'm not asking you to love the genre of music nor am I even trying to convince you to like it. *I only want you to listen to the lyrics for empowerment*.

If it's a song by a man, switch the song around as if it were a woman speaking those words about a man. Remember men are hoes and bitches too, and watch how that changes your attitude towards men.

Song List

-<u>Raining Men by Rihanna / Nicki Minaj</u> (The Power of the Pussy, The Power of Confidence, The Power of Being the Game & Taking Out The Trash, This song covers a lot of the book.)

-<u>We Are Never Ever Getting Back Together</u> – Taylor Swift (The Power of Taking Out The Trash)

-<u>Raining Men by The Weather Girls</u> (Empowers The Super Dater)

-<u>Ho Problems by JT Money </u>(Helps You Leave A Cheater)

-<u>Man, I Feel Like a Woman by Shania Twain </u>(Enjoy Being a Girl)

-<u>That Don't Impress Me Much by Shania Twain </u>(The Power of Selective Attraction)

-<u>Born This Way by Lady Gaga</u> (The Power of Confidence)

-<u>Dirt Off Your Shoulder by Jay-Z </u>(Power of Confidence, People Talking Bad About You...You Can Choose to Let it

Bother You or You Can Choose to Brush It Off)

-Hit Em' Up Style Hit Em' Up Style —— Blu Cantrell
(The Power of Taking Out The Trash)

-Shake You Off Shake You Off —— Mariah Carey
(Controlling Emotions in the End of Relationships)

-Make it Happen Make it Happen —— Mariah Carey (The
Power of Keeping Yourself Busy, Very Important Questions
Assignment)

-Did I Do That? — Mariah Carey (Power of Taking Out
The Trash)

-I Don't Wanna Cry I Don't Wanna Cry —— Mariah Carey
(Power of Taking Out The Trash, Do You Enjoy Being
Sad?)

-Womanizer Womanizer —— Britney Spears (Men Use
Us, Power of Controlling Emotions)

-Can I Get A Fuck You Can I Get A Fuck You —— Jay-Z
(Using Men, Power of Confidence)

-A Little Too Late — Toby KeithA Little Too Late — Toby

Keith (The Power of Taking Out The Trash, Controlling Emotions at the End of Relationships)

-Motivation by Kelly Rowland (Power of Appreciation and The Power of the Pussy, Sexually Rewarding a Man Subconsciously)

-Material Girl by Madonna (Power of Confidence, Power of the Pussy, *Listen to the lyrics, they are very empowering regardless if you are materialistic or not.*)

-Not Gon' Cry Not Gon' Cry by Mary J Blige (Helps get over a BADLY broken heart.)

-U and Ur Hand U and Ur Hand by Pink (The Power of Confidence)

-Fun House by Pink (Going through a divorce? Turn this one up loud! This song is for you.)

-Wide Awake by Katy Perry(If you wish you knew then, what you know now...blast this one loud. Be happy and celebrate the fact that you are now one of few women who can clearly see when a man is trying to use her or take advantage of her. You are wide awake.)

-Cold Hard Bitch by Jet (The Power of The Pussy, The Power of Being the Game)

- Are You Gonna Be My Girl? by Jet (The Power of the Super Dater, The Power of Being the Game)

-The Only Girl In The World by Rihanna (When You Find A Man That Makes You Feel This Way, He's a Keeper!)

-Pussy Real Good by Jackie-O (The Power of the Pussy, This song is the best! You will get a good laugh out of this one.)

-99 Problems by Jay-Z (Flip the Music Around: *"If you're having man problems, I feel bad for you girl, I got 99 problems, but a dick ain't one!"* See how that works. So, the next time you listen to this song, just sing it flipped around and watch how easily you gain empowerment.)

-Don't Trust No N*gga by Khia (Very empowering song but listen at your own risk! It's Explicit.)

- Fighter by Christina Aguilera (The Power of Taking Out the Trash, How Men Use Us, Strength to Get Through A Break Up)

-Songs by Trina: The rap artist Trina empowered me as a young woman. I love her simply for teaching me how to be a strong woman that doesn't take shit from men. I suggest you listen to these songs. However, she is not for the faint of heart. The lyrics are VERY EXPLICIT. Here are some of her most empowering songs:

-N*ggas Ain't Shit_ (The Power of Acting Like A Man, Flipping the Music Around, The Power of Taking Out the Trash, Men Need Us, We Don't Need Them, The Power of Being The Game)

-Watch Your Back (How Men Use Our Emotions Against Us)

-The Baddest Bitch (Power of the Pussy, The Power of Confidence, The Power of Being The Game)

-Don't Trip (The Last Verse is All About How to Use The Power of the Pussy)

-Big Ole' Dick (The Power of Acting Like A Man)

-Always (Power of Appreciation)

-Single Again (The Power of the Super Dater, The Power of

Being The Game, Staying Strong After a Break Up,
Controlling Emotions at the End of Relationships)

**This list would not be complete if I didn't include songs
by Beyonce:**

-Upgrade You (The Power of Being the Game)

-Who Runs the World? (The Power of the Pussy)

-Single Ladies (The Power of Action, The Power of Taking
Out the Trash)

-Cater To You – Destiny's Child (The Power of
Appreciation)

-Best Thing I Never Had
(The Power of Taking out the Trash)

-Irreplaceable
(The Power of Taking Out the Trash)

-Bills, Bills, Bills – Destiny's Child
(The Power of Taking Out The Trash, Spot a Loser)

-<u>Independent Women</u> – Destiny's Child (The Power of Keeping Yourself Busy, Very Important Questions)

-<u>Survivor</u> – Destiny's Child (The Power of Taking Out The Trash, Help Getting Through a Bad Break Up)

Chapter 11

THE POWER OF APPRECIATION

If you follow through on all of the tips in this book, you'll eventually run into your Mr. Right. This won't happen overnight or next month. *In fact, the longer you wait, the better your chances are of finding the best man for you.*

I think we need to be single for several years before deciding to settle down with anyone. We need to fully discover and appreciate who we are as a person, before we mesh our life with someone. You're only young and single once. One day you'll be married and the fun of dating will be a thing of the past. Therefore, you should really enjoy yourself. Get out there and just have FUN.

One day in the midst of all that fun, when you least expect it...you'll meet a special man. The man that has all of the requirements you demand. A man that shows his love through his actions. A man *determined* to beat every other man at the game of winning your heart. He'll pass the Prince Charming test with ease. He's going to be everything you ever wanted and more!

He'll be faithful, respectful, adoring, and simply perfect for you. After having sex with him, he'll still be all of these great things. He won't be a loser, a user, or a cheater. Your family and friends will all like him.

He will have proven himself to be a good man. Now that he's put in all of this hard work, you have some work to do. You have a very important task ahead of you. This task is simple, yet vital to the success of your relationship:

You give him your heart.

This is the guy who is worthy of the prize. All of the emotion you held back, all of the oral sex you held back, all of the nurturing and compassion you held back...let it go. You can now relax and let the love pour out of you onto this man. He deserves it. He worked hard for it. He waited patiently. He treated you right. He didn't use you. This is a good man and he deserves a good woman. Give him your all.

Put that man on a pedestal. Make him feel like "the man." Tell him how much you love and appreciate him. Show him respect and put him above all other men. He won you fair and square. Stand by his side and be his trophy. He deserves the best from you, just like you deserve the best from him. Long lasting, healthy relationships are built on a foundation of mutual respect.

Something Grandma Always Said

There is something my grandmother (who has been married for 50 years) said to me once, "If you want a good husband, you have to be a good wife." I thought that was so sexist, at first. Then it dawned on me that the statement goes both ways. There's an important message behind that statement. If you want a good man in your life, then when you have a good man, you need to be a good woman to him.

Don't cheat on him. Don't disrespect him. Don't treat him like shit. Why do women do that? They get a good man and that's the guy they cheat on or hurt. When you find a man willing to be dedicated to you and who's head over heels in love with you, that's the man you honor with your love. Not the assholes, cheaters, users, and losers.

When you find that good man; save your heart, love, respect, and commitment for him and **only him**. Don't allow any other man to come before him, no matter what. If you do this, you'll never be sad over a man again. You'll be treated well and you'll always have a good man committed to you for life. In addition, only if he's a good man will he get a good woman in return.

This means if at any moment this man starts to fail at being the best man he can be, you shouldn't have a problem walking away and taking all your good love with you. Same goes for you, if at any moment, you start being unfaithful or ungrateful to that good man, he should leave you. You don't deserve a great man if you can't be a great woman in return. So, if you want a good man, when you find him, be good to him.

Communication With Men

When you find your Mr. Right, become his biggest fan. As long as he's being faithful, honest, adoring, and treating you the way you need to be treated; he should know you'll be all of those things to him in return.

Applaud him. Let him know he's a good man. Let him know his kind ways of loving you are appreciated. Thank him when he takes out the trash. Reward him when he does something special for you. Everyone likes a pat on the back. Everyone likes to be told when they're doing a good job.

It is now that you're in a deeply committed relationship that you have to do a few things to keep the relationship on a strong path. When he does something you like, reward him with sex or oral sex. Never have sex with him if he starts slacking somehow. **You don't need to be obvious about this.** Just get to a point where you sexually reward him for good behaviors and sexually punish him for bad behaviors. Do it subliminally, with your pussy powers!

Be open with this man. If he does something you don't like, talk to him and be honest about how you're feeling. Don't keep it bottled inside until you blow up and scream. Don't walk around with anger and an attitude. Just say it in a calm, unheated way. For example; while laying in bed, rub his chest and tell him nicely what it is he did to make you upset and exactly what he can do to fix it. Don't be mean and overcritical about it.

Men respond best to direct instructions. They don't understand the silent treatment or the cold shoulder. Men aren't at all receptive to our anger cues. Of course they figure it out after we've been slamming doors and sucking our teeth all day. But do you really enjoy that style of communication? No. It's a lot easier and less dramatic to just talk about the issue.

Men are very receptive to straight talk, so take advantage of that. It will save you a lot of wasted energy and you'll be amazed at how easily you get what you want. Especially if you're calm and/or sexy when you complain. Stay away from bitching, nagging, and screaming. Chances are he'll bend over backwards to correct the situation. When he does, simply thank him. Or blow him. Your choice.

Nobody's Perfect

As I mentioned earlier, no man is perfect. Some women have issues with maintaining relationships because they're searching for perfection. They'll find something wrong with every guy they date, and they find it impossible to look past negative qualities.

Virtually every man you meet will have some kind of annoying quality. Be cautious and take notice if you've been doing this, because being too picky about the wrong things can lead to a lonely life.

I completely agree you shouldn't settle for less and you should set your standards high. However, what about the day you meet a man that has a majority of the qualities you want? Are you going to let a few imperfections or irritating qualities get in the way of a potentially amazing relationship? A lot of women will and that's why a lot of women are lonely.

You have to understand that in order to have a healthy relationship, with a great man, you're going to have to let some things slide. My man is far from perfect, but his good qualities outweigh his bad qualities, *by far*. So, I chose to let the bad stuff go. I know he's never going to be perfect.

Here is a funny and true story. One day my man farted really loud; like most men do. I must have had PMS or I was at the edge of my patience for his noisy flatulence, because I turned and looked at him with an angry gleam in my eye and rudely said, "Do I have to live with farts for the rest of my life?!" Do you know what this asshole had the nerve to say to me? He calmly replied, "Do I have to live with cellulite for the rest of my life?"

I backed off. You know something? He was right. It was in that moment I realized if I wanted a man to love me unconditionally and see past my faults, then I would need to do the same for him. When you find a good man that meets a majority of your standards and treats you well, try your hardest to look past his faults.

You will ***never*** find a man without irritating

qualities — they don't exist. So, you might as well learn to accept the man whose bad qualities are ones you can deal with. When his faults irritate you and get under your skin, remember that *you have faults, too*. We all want to be accepted for who we are, whether that means being a gassy guy or having cellulite on your thighs. Nobody's perfect.

Wise Women Have Back Up Plans

Now, don't ever begin to get stupid because you're in love. You can let your emotions out now that you're in love, but you still need to be on point. If this great guy suddenly starts being not so great, don't hesitate to cut him off! You need to be prepared to up and leave him at ANYTIME. This means you always have a back up plan.

Wise women have back up plans. The very first time he ever cheats on you, hits you or does anything unacceptable; leave him. You don't ask questions. You don't cry or grovel in front of him. Control your emotions and leave him forever.

You can't have a man cheat on you, go back with him, and expect everything to be great again. He ruined it. You have to make him suffer for his mistake. If you don't, he'll start to make mistakes more often. You have to keep him scared of losing you. He must know you won't put up with shit, and that you're *not afraid to leave him.*

Now, chances are if you follow the book, you won't

have these problems. This poor man had to work SO HARD to get you. He had to play that game SO GOOD to win that prize.

The harder you work for something, the more you appreciate it. You made him work so hard for his big prize, he won't ever want to let you go! When you play exactly by the rules of this book, you'll end up with a man that will dedicate his life to making you happy.

Chapter 12

THE POWER OF THE UTERUS

Having a vagina comes with a HUGE responsibility. That responsibility lies right there inside of you. It's your uterus. The final power is about controlling two very important decisions in your life:

WHEN you get pregnant

and

WHO you allow to father your children.

These two decisions are completely under

YOUR CONTROL.

If you don't know the answers to these two questions, then now is the time to really think about your ideal scenario. Figure out when you would prefer to start having kids. Think about the kind of man you would want to father your children.

These are some of the most important decisions you will ever have to make in your lifetime. What's even more important is making sure *you* are the one who controls these decisions. Don't allow fate or the men in your life to make these decisions for you.

Some of you are already maintaining a tight control over your uterus. If you're a pro at keeping that thing locked down like a prison cell, that's great! Keep it up. But some of us…not so much. It's time to address this situation because it's becoming a big problem for us.

As women, we need to respect the responsibility of having a uterus, and we haven't been doing a very good job at it. We need to accept the reality that a majority of unplanned pregnancies are our own fault.

Yes, I just said that.

We put ourselves into bad situations by not taking the necessary amount of responsibility for our own body parts. We've been too sloppy with our miracle makers! God gave us this awesome privilege and what do we do with it? Go around passing out miracles to men who are unworthy and unappreciative.

Every day men are impregnating us and then leaving us to deal with the responsibility on our own. It has forced women to step up and become Mothers and Fathers — all while working a full time job. It's not healthy for us, it's not healthy for society; but more importantly, it's not healthy for our children.

We like to blame it all on dead beat dads, but we are the ones **ALLOWING** dead beat men to lay down with us! Don't get me wrong, men need to step up as well. This isn't about giving them a free pass for being piece of shit fathers. The problem is we can't control what men do (or don't do), but we can control what we do. That's where the power lies, right there in that uterus of yours.

Accidents happen; babies are made and lives get interrupted in the process. I understand this is a part of life. In fact, it's the harsh reality of being a woman. I'm not downing any woman who has had an accidental pregnancy, or who is a single mother and/or a teen mother. In fact, you're probably a wiser and stronger woman because of that experience.

I give you 100% respect, because I know it was probably one of the hardest things you have ever had to go through. However, that's not to say that single mothers and/or teen mothers wouldn't agree with everything I'm saying. I think it's safe to say that at least 90% would agree and pass along these same words of wisdom.

That's not to say that I'm perfect, either. Accidental pregnancies are a fact of life. I've had one. It was a very tough time in my life. I'm a stay at home mother with a supportive partner, and it was a very difficult experience for me.

I can't even imagine the stress of doing it on my own or with a man who wasn't 100% supportive. So, this goes for me, as well as every one of you: **We all need to be more pro-active about preventing unwanted pregnancies.**

It's Easier Than You Think

Women get pregnant. Sometimes, very easily. A lot easier than we think, until it actually happens. We can have sex one time and get pregnant. ONCE. One accident is all it takes. ONE!!! Think about what that really means.

Unfortunately, we don't ever stop to think about what that really means until we're sitting on the toilet crying over a positive pregnancy test. It's in that *exact moment* that you realize: "That was a lot easier than I thought."

The even bigger and harsher realization is that it's too late to take it back. That's when the panic sets in. Your little *one-time* mistake just changed your life *forever*. Before you know it, you're locked down for the next 20 years working HARD every day to take care of your child. Raising a child is a full time job. Shit, it's more than a full time job. It's a 365 days a year, 24 hours a day, 7 days a week, never ending HARD job.

Personal goals, dreams, and accomplishments temporarily fly out the window. Your life is no longer your own and it' changes forever once you have children. By being in full control of your reproductive organs, you're maintaining full control of your life, your future, and your child's future.

Make A Bold Statement to the Men in Your Life

By being extremely responsible and careful with your body, you are subconsciously making a bold statement to the men in your life. You're saying: "When I do decide to have children; they'll be with a man who's going to marry me, take care of me, and hold my hand throughout the entire process." It also says, "I'm very picky about who I share my DNA with."

This is a very empowering and respectable statement to make to the men in your life. How do you make this statement if it's subconscious? **You make it silently, by taking the lead when it comes to your body.** Instead of doing any of these naïve alternatives:

-Going with the flow until an accident happens.

-Irresponsible slip-ups (Missing a pill, getting a shot late, etc...)

-Leaving the responsibility up to the man.

-Purposely wanting to get pregnant by some loser. (Don't be a dumb ass.)

-Or the worst one: Trusting a man's opinion about YOUR body, which is usually falling for a mixture of classic excuses such as:

"I'll pull out."

"I can't get girls pregnant."

"I had a surgery when I was five, I'm not fertile."

"Just this once? Pleeeease?"

Don't be the fool. Stand up for yourself. Show men you respect your body. You do this by being **100% dedicated** to using birth control and condoms until you find a man that really deserves to have a baby with you. Do not make these crucial mistakes:

Don't get pregnant because you lost focus in a moment of passion. This is when it usually happens, so be prepared. Don't say I didn't warn you! Be ready to control yourself and say no in the heat of the moment if you don't have the proper protection. Don't allow the passion to get you pregnant. This is the most common way we end up accidentally pregnant. Damn that heat of the moment passion

That uncontrollable passion usually occurs when you're ovulating. You release pheromones that get your man all hot and bothered (even more than usual). Plus, you feel all hot and horny too, because of all the hormones. That's why it can be so hard to stop. So, be careful!

Don't allow yourself to get pregnant by men who don't treat you well. You'll only be setting yourself up for heartache and a ton of stress. This can happen in an instant, so you must be aware and cautious at all times.

Don't allow men to convince you that pulling out will work. It doesn't. It may work the first few times, or the first few months, but eventually you'll end up pregnant. It happens all the time, so be careful.

Don't rely on Plan B as a back up. One out of eight women will still get pregnant. (I know this is a fact from personal experience. I learned the hard way about trusting Plan B.)

Don't get too drunk and make a huge mistake. This is another culprit of the unplanned pregnancy. A lot of babies are made in a drunken moment of passion. If you're getting drunk and being sloppy and irresponsible, you're going to end up pregnant!

Don't use cheap condoms. Condoms break. If you have to use cheap ones, double them up. Even quality condoms will break if you get too dry and rough, so be careful. Keep back up condoms or lube to avoid it drying up and breaking.

Get on birth control and be responsible about taking it correctly: Be pro-active about getting on birth control and be disciplined about taking it correctly. If it's pills, take them every day. If you miss a day or two, then don't have sex without a condom for at least one month. You CAN get pregnant by missing a pill or two throughout the month. If you're on the shot, make sure you get your next shot on time. If you get your shot late, use protection, don't assume you're protected.

By utilizing the power of your uterus, you are also utilizing other powers, such as the power of being the game. You're not making it easy for men to get you pregnant. You're being picky and choosy about who you allow to impregnate you.

This will give you control over men instead of being dependent upon them. It will also enable you to live a happier and healthier life; simply by staying in control of who gets you pregnant and when you allow them to do it.

If you've been one bit irresponsible about this, I'm here to tell you to tighten up! It'll happen a lot quicker than you expect. If you're young and you've been having unprotected sex, cut it out. You'll be knocked up and pregnant before you know it! Sometimes we just need to be reminded how easily one can become pregnant. Pulling out won't work every time. Plan B won't work every time.

Condoms break.

If you've been thinking you can't get pregnant because it's been years and you're not pregnant yet, think again. BAM. It happens like lighting! Just because it hasn't happened yet, doesn't mean it won't happen tomorrow.

My Rude Awakening

I'm sure you've learned all of these things in Sex Ed. and you may even be thinking, "Whatever, lady. I'm not stupid. I'm not going to get pregnant." I used to say the same thing. Until recently.

I was accidentally knocked up by my husband and I had a rude awakening. I had to learn the hard way: It's not a good idea to have unprotected sex when you're wasted and not on birth control. Hey, it was just one time!

We were always very responsible. Both of my previous pregnancies were planned. I honestly didn't think I would happen to get pregnant from that one little mistake. Besides, I was going to take a Plan B the next day to be on the safe side. Guess what? Plan B didn't work.

Turns out that I didn't read the fine print. One out of eight women will still get pregnant after using Plan B. So there I was, having my third baby, this time, through an unplanned pregnancy. Take it from me, don't rely solely on Plan B or any other method. Have back up plans, use double protection, do whatever it takes to control your uterus!

The only reason I wanted to include this chapter is because I think women who control their uterus will always have an upper hand when it comes to loving relationships. You should especially listen to this chapter's advice if you're young, in a bad relationship, unprepared; or all three.

Stay on top of your birth control. Take responsibility. Don't listen to men or take their advice about your body. If he says he'll pull out and that it will work, tell him that jacking off works too! If he says he shoots blanks and never got a girl pregnant before, tell him you're not going to be the first. Be firm and take the lead when it comes to protecting yourself.

The Strongest Creatures

I'm not saying that having a baby will destroy your life, or that if you have a baby with somebody who isn't 100% percent there, that you won't be able to do it. I think women are the strongest creatures on the planet. We adapt and we make it happen, no matter what.

It honestly doesn't matter what obstacle comes in our way, we will overcome it for the love of our babies. If a man comes into our life and then leaves or half asses his responsibility, we will handle the situation and take care of our children by ourselves. But just because we *can*, doesn't mean we *should*.

Pussy and the Evolution of Man

Ladies, we have the ultimate ability to change the way men have been behaving by making it an honor and a privilege to make a baby with us. We need to be the generation of women that steps up and says: "Enough is enough. Men must prove they're responsible and worthy of being fathers or they won't be fathers."

We can only do this if we come together and collectively control our uteruses. We need to make a bold statement as women: **We are now very picky about who gets us pregnant and when we allow them to get us pregnant.**

This will force the male species to evolve...

Pussy has that much power!

There's something wrong with society. We have become numb to the alarming rate of young mothers, single mothers, and dead beat dads. Even us older women, we should be ashamed that we don't reach out and encourage the younger generation to wait and be responsible. Young girls need to step up too, maintain control, and stop getting pregnant at such a young age.

We need to live out our lives, wait until we're older and have a baby with somebody who's going to be there for a lifetime. **If you control your uterus, you'll control who your child's father will be and what kind of life you and your future children will have. That is an amazingly important thing to control!**

That's why the power of the uterus needs to be a top priority for any woman. Don't wait until it's too late to take this advice. Be smart and be in control of your body. Be a role model to other women, especially young women. If we come together to make this change, if we collectively take responsibility for our bodies, we'll force men to be better. We'll force them to evolve. **You** have that much power!

CONCLUSION

I wrote this book to help my fellow ladies learn how to get what they want from men. Whether that's love, marriage, respect or just empowerment; everyone needs a little direction to get what they want or to become the person they want to be.

I hope my book provided you with that direction. These same techniques have worked in my personal life. I, myself, was once confused and manipulated by men until I these techniques. The powers helped me find a wonderful man who is head over heels in love with me. He is literally my best friend and my soul mate. I want to share my story with you in hopes that it will encourage you, and also serve as proof there really are great men out there.

Like a lot of girls, I had a high school sweetheart. He wasn't the worst guy in the world, but he definitely wasn't the best. When I was 19, I finally found the strength to leave him. I found the strength in wanting to be single and free while I was still in my youth. Besides, I was only going to be young once. So, I left... after four years. It was after this break up that I discovered the powers and started using them.

From that time until the age of 23; I was single, free, and loving it! I went to college and I was also determined to get hired at a radio station (my five year goal). Within a year I got hired as a phone girl at Power 96, which is a big radio station in Miami, Florida. It was at this point in my life that I was solely concentrating on learning everything I could at the station. I was building my radio career. I wasn't worried about a man, dating, or finding a new boyfriend.

I wasn't interested in a relationship and I think it really showed. That's where I learned the power of keeping yourself busy really did work, because it wasn't until I was focused on a career and *wanted* to be single that the men flocked to me.

Well, then I started doing some online dating, just to have guys there to take me out when I was bored. That's when I learned how to use the power of the super dater. I thought I had men flocking to me before, you should have seen after I started doing online dating. I had so many men lined up to date me that the choices were endless. It was a smorgasbord of men just waiting to take me out on a date!

In the midst of all this serial dating and career building, I met a guy at a gas station (of all places, believe it or not). I was pumping gas and this guy and his friends were hanging out of a car, hootin' and hollerin', "hey baby, hey sexy." Now, usually I would ignore this type of pervert nonsense behavior, but one of the guys caught my eye. He was cute and had a lot of tattoos, which was a total turn-on to me.

He caught my eye, so I actually decided to approach the car full of drooling pervs. The tattoo guy and I talked for a minute and then we exchanged numbers. We started hanging out and he was actually a lot of fun. We had a lot of things in common. I was a loud and crazy person, and he was just as loud and crazy as I was.

He really entertained me and made me laugh. Something no other man was able to do (and one of the important things on my "dream man" list was a good sense of humor). I really had a good time with him, but I controlled my emotions and stayed single. I wasn't looking for a boyfriend and I let him know this from the beginning. I was using the power of being the game and guess what? It worked.

My rejection didn't stop him. He waited patiently and continued to pursue me. That was proof to me that when a man really likes you, he'll continue to pursue you even after you've rejected him.

Eventually, I got aggressive and told him we could remain friends or we could be nothing at all. I thought that would be the end of it, but he said he'd rather have me as his friend than nothing at all. After that, he respectively backed off. Well, we all know there's nothing a man likes more than a pussy challenge! So, he waited…

It was around that same time I discovered the power of selective attraction. I had all of these guys at my feet, but after a few years of that I became more interested in quality over quantity. That's when I realized why it's so important to be attracted to the way men treated me, above all other things. This weeded out a bunch of guys, because as we all know, the majority of men won't treat us well.

Something was different about tattoo guy. He treated me really well and he was so good to me. He was *determined* to beat every other man at the 'who can win Kara's love' game. He passed multiple Prince Charming tests. In fact, he was the only man that ever passed them with flying colors. He treated his Mom and Grandmother with the utmost respect. He met a majority of the qualities I had on my list and he wasn't a user or a loser. I thought to myself, "I just may have a winner here."

He pursued me for eight months before I finally gave in. I'm sure he had his girls on the side during that time, just like I had my flings. He used those girls for sex, but I was the woman he was in love with and actively pursuing.

After three and a half years of being single, I realized I'd found someone worthy of my love and respect. This man was worth settling down with, so *I decided* to be his girlfriend. *I chose him*, instead of it being the other way around.

You *can* have the relationship you desire with a wonderful man, *if* you stick to using the powers. The proof is in the pudding. I've been with tattoo guy for over eleven years. We have three beautiful daughters together and he's an absolutely amazing father! (This was another thing at the top of my requirements list.)

He works very hard so I can be a stay-at-home mother. (Something I clearly and sweetly asked him to do for me.) He's in love with me and I'm in love with him, even after all of these years.

He's everything I ever dreamed of a husband being and more! Let me tell you something else, I'm not as sexy as I used to be, either. I'm overweight after having three children. He still treats me as if I'm a sexy goddess. I never have to feel uncomfortable around him because of my weight. I've never worried about him cheating on me or leaving me for another woman, EVER. I told you good men do exist!

The most important factor is I appreciate him. All of the love and respect he gives me, I return to him. I'll never let another man come between us. He's my king and I'll treat him with that respect as long as he continues to treat me with the same respect.

Lastly, I'm not afraid to leave him and he knows it. He knows if he cheated on me, I'd leave him without a second thought. I'd be devastated and it would crush me, but I wouldn't stick around for it to happen again.

I used the powers in this book and I have a good man and a wonderful relationship. Stick to the powers and I promise, you'll find your perfect man too. You can read this book a hundred times, but it's up to you to master the techniques and actually practice them in real life.

You can do this. I did it. It works. It may take time to adjust and get used to doing things a new way. You may even hit a few bumps in the road along the way. However, eventually you'll get comfortable with these techniques and you'll be so happy you know them.

Some women never learn the tricks in this book. You're now one of few women who understand men. You know how they think and why they do what they do. You can now use what you know to flip things around and beat men at their own game.

I also want to invite you to join The Power of the Pussy's Facebook page and follow me on Twitter. I update Twitter and Facebook with funny and motivational material every single day. I'm very involved and interactive on these accounts. So please, feel free to join in on the fun on Twitter @KaraKing. I follow back all of my readers, just shoot me a tweet and say hello, and I will follow you back. On Facebook, you can find me at http://www.facebook.com/ThePoweroftheP.

I wish you luck in your love life and may you find your perfect Prince Charming. Thank you for reading my book and please feel free to send me an email at makemenloveyou@aol.com or leave a review on Amazon.com or Goodreads.com when you've found your man. I love to hear success stories!

Assignments Section

The next few pages are the assignments throughout the book.

Things I Hate About Him

Write down all of the things that make you mad about this man. From the little insignificant things to the big things. You want to write down anything and everything that ever bothered you. Personality traits, physical traits, and even situations that occurred during your relationship need to be on the list. All of the bad stuff. ALL OF IT. When you're having a hard time, pull out this list and remember why you don't want or need that man in your life.

1.
2.
3.
4.
5.
6.
7.
8.
9.
10.
11.
12.
13.
14.

15.

16.

17.

18.

19

20.

What Do You Want From Men That You Have Been Unable To Obtain in the Past?

Take this time to write down exactly what you want to accomplish with men. What do you really want from a man, that you've been unable to get in the past? Is it commitment? Is it honesty? Gifts? Dates? Marriage? These are going to be your demands. You shouldn't settle down with any man until he's willing to give you exactly what you desire. If he isn't willing, then you'll need to cut your losses, control your emotions, and move on to the next man.

1. Honesty
2. Adoration
3. Commitment

My Offerings

Make a list of at least ten things you have to offer, even more if you can get them down, but at least ten. These attributes can't be physical or sexual. Don't write down, "I have a nice ass." These have to be personality traits, talents, goals, achievements, etc…

1.

2.

3.

4.

5.

6.

7.

8.

9.

10.

My Perfect Dream Man

Write down ten things you really want in a man. This is different from the assignment earlier that asks, 'what do you want from men that you have been unable to receive in the past.' This list is all about your dream man. If you could design your perfect guy, what type of qualities would he have? You can list physical, sexual, emotional or financial attributes. Don't forget to be reasonable. You can come up with as many things as you want, but narrow it down to the TOP TEN things your perfect man would have.

1.

2.

3.

4.

5.

6.

7.

8.

9.

10.

Very Important Questions

Some of you have this stuff figured out already. For those of you who don't, take a moment to think about what you want from life. Think about what you want your future to be like. Don't be afraid to dream big! Answer these very important questions:

Where would you like to see yourself in one year?

Set some one year goals:

Where would you like to see yourself in five years?

Set some five year goals:

Where would you like to see yourself in ten years?

Set some ten year goals:

What is your dream career?

How much money do you want to earn per year?

Write in detail the work that you need do to reach each of your goals:

Work needed for the 1 year goal:

Work needed for the 5 year goal:

Work needed for the 10 year goal:

For those of you that have these things figured out already, that's great! That's one less thing you need to worry about when dealing with men. However, some of you are wandering aimlessly. You're not working towards anything and that will never help you get what you want from men as per the advice in this book. That will only make you dependent upon men (the exact opposite result!).

So, set some goals and work hard towards these goals. Whatever it is, I promise you can accomplish it. When it seems impossible just remember that anything worth having in life is going to take some hard work. When you get discouraged, remember that you'll reach your goals a lot faster than you think it will take to get there.

Besides, if you never start, you'll never get there. Make sure they are practical and achievable goals, but *do not be afraid to set big goals*. Whatever it is you chose to accomplish, I promise, you can do it if you put your mind to it. Always believe in yourself.

BONUS MATERIAL

Using Men: Sugar Daddies and Sponsors

If you are offended by women using men for financial gain, you may want to skip over this section.

I was getting so much hateful feedback for including this section. I think people were misunderstanding my reasons for including this section. This section is simply an FYI. It's not a required part of the book, so I decided to move it to the back of the book as a bonus section. However, using men for money *is* a power that the pussy beholds. Therefore, I would be doing my readers (and the rich men that want to pamper them) an injustice to leave out this very important information.

Before I get into using men for money, I have a few things I want to say about this controversial topic. As women, we have become conditioned by society to believe certain things and behave a certain way. Men haven't been conditioned to believe these same things. For example, why is it when a woman uses a man for money, she's labeled as a gold digging whore, both by men *and* women?

However, when a man uses women for sex, he's revered as a "player" and "the man." Sure, it's frowned upon as well, but nowhere near the extent that women are looked down upon for doing the same type of "bad behavior." Do you think these double standards are an accident? I sure don't. Society dictates how we should behave. Society is run by men. This is NOT an accident.

We've been tricked! We have been **man**ipulated to act and think a certain way THAT BENEFITS MEN!!! When women try to go against the grain, they are criticized. The only way you can escape this patriarchal bullshit is to reject it. Don't allow society to guilt you.

See it for what it is: Men trying to keep us from doing the same things they do. They have us under control. They like it that way. They don't want us to join in on the fun. They don't want us to wake up and figure this out. Of course they're going to bad mouth you for doing anything other than what they have conditioned you to do! They don't want their own games played on them. Using men is simply spoon feeding them their own hypocritical bullshit and if they don't like it...too bad!

They have many names: sugar daddies, paymasters, sponsors...etc. Whatever you want to call them, there are men everywhere that are ready and willing to be used by you. I know. Using men is wrong. Whatever...fuck that! We can argue about the morality of using people, but I'm not here to judge people and talk about what's right and wrong.

I'm here to be honest and informative. Here is the honesty: men use us, so fuck them, use them back! Here is the informative part: Men are so easy to use and you can get all kinds of things from them. Woo hoo! I love the power of the pussy!

There are different ways you can use men. You can use them for simple things, such as bringing you a nice lunch to work or you can take it all the way to the extreme and marry a rich man for money. We already discussed filler dates and using men to entertain us. Let's dig deeper and discuss using men for financial gain.

The first thing you must know is that there are men that can be used and there are men that can't be used. The men that can be used usually fall into one of three categories: older men, foreign men, and men desperate to get laid. (Which are usually nerdy/ugly guys or guys that are in love with you.) Find a man in all three categories with a lot of money — jackpot!

All jokes aside, these men won't be good looking or the type of guys you would normally date. Paymasters, sponsors, and sugar daddies are men you would never date in a million years, but that's where you win! When you find a man in one of those categories, or he finds you, **he has to like you**. If he does, then flirt a tiny bit and act like you're interested; even though you're not. Once these men want you, they're willing to impress you.

Once they're willing to impress you, you can begin to get away with asking for stuff. After a few days/dates/conversations, then try to ask for something. Start off small. Ask for some money to fill up your gas tank. If he does it easily, he's a sponsor!

If you're feeling uncomfortable about this, start off

with using men for dates (aka free dinners). Once you're comfortable with the thought of using a man, you can move on to asking for other things. When you're ready to proceed with bigger items, you have to come at the man in a needy way. You have make him feel like you need him to rescue you. When a man likes a woman, he'll rush to her side to be the man that solves her problems, remember.

So, let's say you hang onto a few guys that you don't like, but they all like you. Well, then you have an arsenal of men at your disposal ready to say, "how high?" every time you ask them to jump! What do you want them to do for you? Buy you an outfit? Fix your car? Take you out for lunch? Ask and you shall receive. Now, if you don't receive or he makes an issue out of it, politely cut him off and move on to the next man.

Some men will give you things without effort, others are cheap and won't even give you a dollar. Don't waste your time trying to use a man that won't allow himself to be used. You are now like the guys who are going to try to use you for sex. When they try and can't get it, they'll just go away because they know you can't be used. They won't waste anymore time or effort. You have to start thinking with that same selfish mentality: "If I'm not getting what I want, then I'm out of here and on to the next one."

The final and most important part about using men is that you **NEVER** have to have sex or do anything sexual to get what you want. If a man is buying you things and he gets frustrated because you're not having sex with him, just leave him alone. Most of them will get to this point at some time; some quicker than others.

Some will allow you to use them for years, without ever asking for anything in return. Some will just want to show you off to their friends and family. Let him. If he's a good sponsor, then be a gracious receiver. When you do find a good one, respect him and make him feel like you enjoy his company. Don't be rude to him and don't be a bitch to him. There's no need to be disrespectful, insulting, or hurtful.

Most men know when they're being used, but some don't mind if they are being used in a respectful way by a pretty, younger woman they can show off. Remember, men enjoy the presence of a woman and some guys won't mind paying for that presence. If you feel bad about using men, then don't do it! Or simply do it with a man that knows what your intentions are upfront. Then you really aren't doing anything wrong. Trust me, a lot of men don't mind. He may thoroughly enjoy spoiling you.

Most are probably thinking they might have a chance at sex if they keep shelling out cash. Their intentions aren't important to you. What is important to you is getting what you want. If he isn't going to give it to you, you're going to find a man that will. It's time for you to be selfish. It's time for you to be the one using men, instead of them using you.

Have fun being a girl. If you want to use men, then do it and *do it without guilt*. If you find it to be morally wrong, ***then don't do it***. To each their own. However, if you would like to give it a try, I suggest reading "A GOAL Digger's Guide: How To Get What You Want Without Giving It Up" by Baje Fletcher (Don't get caught with that book!) Then start at one of these websites below. Between that book and these sites, you'll easily find men ready and willing to be used by you.

www.SugarDaddyForMe.com

www.SugarDaddie.com

~Boys Are Toys~
HAVE FUN OUT THERE!!!

&

ALWAYS REMEMBER
YOU
HAVE THE POWER.

THE END

Need More Advice?
Now Available!

The Power of the Pussy:
Part Two

Marriage, Divorce, Relationship, and
Dating Advice for Women

Whether You're Single, Married, or Divorced…
You Have The Power!

In the follow-up to the best selling dating advice book, "The Power of the Pussy", Kara King delves further into the controversial subject of Pussy Power. In this book you'll discover unique and compelling advice specifically designed to conquer a variety of real life issues that women may face when dealing with men. The Power of the Pussy Part Two will help you:

- Discover powers that men have and use this knowledge to your advantage.
- Draw men to you naturally and effortlessly.
- Heal from a divorce or bad break-up and come out of it better than ever!
- Use your powers within a marriage to re-ignite the flame or change the dynamics of the relationship.
- Learn tips and tricks to keep a good man head over heels in love with you, eager to remain faithful, and

happy to stand by your side for life.

- Overcome baby daddy drama, rejection, and other real life issues that other dating advice books won't dare discuss!

The Power of the Pussy has been hailed the ultimate must-read dating guide for women of all ages. The first book laid the foundation, while Part Two digs deeper into the world of feminine power. "The Power of the Pussy: Part Two" will make you laugh, leave you feeling empowered, and enable you to deal with anything a man throws your way!

Get your copy today!
Now available on Amazon and Barnes and Noble.

CPSIA information can be obtained at www.ICGtesting.com
Printed in the USA
LVOW12s0226020715

444704LV00015B/137/P